SOULSHAPING

Creating Compassionate Children

KIMBERLY SOWELL

Birmingham, Alabama

New Hope® Publishers
P. O. Box 12065
Birmingham, AL 35202-2065
www.newhopepublishers.com
New Hope Publishers is a division of WMU®.

Printed in the United States of America.

Library of Congress Cataloging-in-Publication Data
Sowell, Kimberly.
Soul shaping : creating compassionate children / Kimberly Sowell.
p. cm.
ISBN 978-1-59669-276-3 (sc)
1. Mothers--Religious life. 2. Parenting--Religious aspects--Christianity. 3. Mother and child--Religious aspects--Christianity. 4. Compassion in children--Religious aspects--Christianity. I. Title.

BV4529.18.S69 2011
248.8'431--dc22

2010037137

ISBN-10: 1-59669-276-6
ISBN-13: 978-1-59669-276-3
N104139 • 0111 • 3M1

This book is dedicated
to my precious kingdom-hearted kids:

Julia Summer Sowell
Jason William Sowell
John Mark Sowell

May you run swiftly for Jesus.

Table of Contents

Introduction

As my mind raced through a mental list of all the miles I had to run that day, completing this errand and that chore, I only half listened to the announcers talking on the Christian radio station playing in my minivan. My young son asked, "Why those people not have nothing?" (That's toddler talk for "Why don't those people have anything?") My mind tuned in to the announcers as they talked about young mothers in need of help at the local crisis pregnancy care center.

"Sometimes people aren't able to buy things they need, and God wants us to help take care of them, sweetie. That helps us show them that God loves them." After my standard mommy textbook response, I went back to my mental to-do list.

After we returned home, my son disappeared to do what I thought was some much anticipated playtime. Moments later, he returned with his fists filled with something shiny. "Here, Mommy. This is for the people who don't have nothing. I want to help them. OK?" He opened up his chubby fingers to reveal every coin he owned, eager to give all he had to help others in need. I stopped dead in my tracks and scooped up my little boy. His heart had grown a little that day, and mine had too.

What makes a little boy decide to empty his piggy bank and hand over his treasure to help people he's never met? It's the same quality of goodness we see in the helping hands of the good Samaritan, or the compassion of the woman who washed the feet of Jesus with her tears and wiped them with her hair. That goodness in my son was a small speck of godliness, a gift of the Lord as He pours His love directly into the heart of a little boy at such a tender age to draw him unto the Savior.

I had little to do with my son's act of kindness and giving. Like all mothers on any given day, I was busy doing the work that keeps a household functioning, and my limited attention span was focused on the tasks at hand. I had chosen to expose my family to what is wholesome through piping Christian radio into our vehicle, that's all; just a simple "as for me and my house" sort of decision. But while I was driving around town, completing those tasks that had to be done for my family's welfare, God was at work in my son. Our Lord will always be the supreme Teacher in every "God moment" we'll ever experience with our children, whether we're being intentional as moms, or we're blessed because God slips into the day a growing moment that we never saw coming.

Are you a kingdom-minded mom? With God's help, you can raise kingdom-minded kids. It sounds like a tough task, especially in the me-oriented culture our children will grow up in, but mothers throughout the ages have been able to raise godly children despite their society's temptations and the common weakness of all flesh. God's love and truth transcends all time, overcomes all evil, and reaches down to guide little children. You can be an agent of that love and truth. You can raise children who embrace a lifestyle to seek first God's kingdom and His righteousness. You can be a kingdom-minded mom! May God mark your journey with spiritual growth, wisdom, strength, victories for the kingdom, and lots and lots of belly laughs.

Kimberly

> *"But seek first the kingdom of God and His righteousness, and all these things shall be added to you."*
> (Matthew 6:33)

And Jesus came and spoke to them, saying, "All authority has been given to Me in heaven and on earth. Go therefore and make disciples of all the nations, baptizing them in the name of the Father and of the Son and of the Holy Spirit, teaching them to observe all things that I have commanded you; and lo, I am with you always, even to the end of the age." Amen.
(Matthew 28:18–20)

Are You a Missionary?

Mommy, what's a missionary?" I've taken courses about the missions field, I've studied about missions, and I've even written about missionaries, but I struggled to answer the question in a way that would satisfy my daughter's childlike understanding of the world.

After much thought and probably some very perplexed expressions on my face, I answered, "A missionary is someone who will go where God asks him to go and will do what God asks him to do to help people and to teach them about Jesus coming to save us from our sins." Surely that would be enough to satisfy Julia's mind, I thought, but her next question took my breath away.

"Mommy, are you a missionary?" My first consideration was to say that I'm not, comparing myself to my many beloved missionary friends who are serving around the world. But then I thought about the definition I had just given Julia. Before I could respond, Julia intersected my thoughts.

"Mommy, you go where Jesus wants you to go, right? And you help people. And you tell people about Jesus. . . so, aren't you a missionary, Mommy?"

The men and women of God who have given their lives to vocational missions in the United States and around the world are fulfilling a high calling indeed, and we admire and appreciate their many sacrifices to the cause of Jesus Christ. But in a sense, all of us who have Jesus as our Lord and Savior have been called to go, to share the good news of Jesus, and to make disciples. Some of us are called to be missionaries vocationally, but all Christians are called to honor God and His cause throughout our days—whether we're doing it by conducting evangelistic soccer camps in Brazil, introducing children to the Bible in Niger, or being salt and light around the water cooler at work and at home with our families.

Your example of fulfilling the Great Commission given by Jesus Christ in Matthew 28:18–20 will have a profound impact on your child's approach to missions work. A hands-off approach that puts all missions work onto the backs of missionaries makes being a missionary a job. A hands-on approach that embraces missions work as the high calling of every Christian makes being a missionary a lifestyle.

I ended that conversation with Julia by asking her if she would go where Jesus sent her, to help people and tell them about Jesus. She and I agreed that we are missionaries in our hometown. How about it? Are *you* a missionary, Mommy?

Heavenly Father, I want to fulfill the call of Jesus to go and make disciples. Teach me to be Your hands and feet, and may my children see in me the heart of a missionary for Your glory. Amen.

Reflection questions:

1. Do you consider yourself to be a kingdom-minded mom? What does that mean in your life?

2. Before Jesus gave the commission to go and tell, He first said that He had all authority in heaven and on earth. How does Christ's authority affect your desire to fulfill His calling?

3. Read Acts 1:8. What other information do you glean from this verse about God's calling in the life of every Christian to adopt a missions lifestyle?

"As missionaries, we desired to involve our sons as much in our ministries as possible. When it's important to the parents, it's important to the children. Now, with a 17- and 20-year-old, missions is a lifestyle. We're sending them off on their missions trips."
Janet Erwin, editor, Missions Mosaic *magazine*

Then King David said to Ornan, "No, but I will surely buy it for the full price, for I will not take what is yours for the Lord, *nor offer burnt offerings with that which costs me nothing."*
(1 Chronicles 21:24)

The Cash Register

We do it every year, and it still hasn't gotten any easier. We're going to keep doing it, though, and I have hope that one day my children will start to "get it." As Christmastime approaches, the children and I pull out all of their toys to decide which ones we need to throw away, which toys we will keep, and which ones we will give away. My children have difficulty discerning between what should be thrown away and what should be given away; they have a tendency to pull out what is broken, boring, or thoroughly worn out, and these are the things they would gladly give away to the poor. The toys that are shiny and noisy, even if they are rarely played with, the children refuse to give away. Only after much begging, pleading, bargaining, and a tad of threatening do the children finally agree to part with a respectable pile of toys.

I'm starting to believe there's hope for this painful exercise we do each year. The last time our family picked through the toys, I shamelessly gave the children a lengthy lecture on the spirit of giving. "Children, what if you were the ones receiving used toys as presents this year? Look at what you've placed in your giveaway pile, and then look at what you're keeping. Are these the things you would want to receive?" Little heads shook left and right, and out poked their bottom lips. "Could you give away just one toy that you really enjoy playing with, something special that would make another little girl or boy happy?"

My daughter's eyes began to scan the room. She glanced over several toys I had hoped she would pick, good toys in excellent condition that for whatever reason had never really struck her fancy. Instead, she slowly walked over to one of her favorite toys, and she handed it to me. "Here, Mommy. I will give away my cash register." No, not the cash register! She had done a lot of chores to earn that cash register from the toy store, and she had spent countless hours playing with it. I knew how much I had paid for it, and it was one of my favorites too!

My daughter had done exactly what I had asked her to do, and I knew the Lord was pleased. The more she talked about how much fun the toy would bring to the child who would receive it, the more joyful her heart became, and soon she was almost giddy about giving away her prized possession. I started to feel a bit giddy myself. I had given my children an award-winning lecture about the spirit of giving, and through my daughter's actions, I was faced with my own personal selfishness. Once I repented, my heart was filled with joy like Julia's. Later that evening, I went through my closet a second time for clothes to give away. I had already sorted out the clothing that was starting to look worn, but that evening I pulled out some items that were in great shape and still in style, hoping to bring a smile to the face of a mother who needed the kindness of a stranger.

Reflect on the words of King David above, and apply his attitude to your family's spirit of giving. When you donate items to the needy, whether it's toys, clothing, or food, your gifts are given as unto the Lord. Jesus said that when we extend our hands to the poor, it's as if we're blessing Him (Matthew 25:34–40). Are you giving your leftover, worn out, broken down junk to honor the Lord, or are you giving sacrificially?

Father, You have blessed our family in so many ways. Give us a spirit of giving joyfully and generously, as unto You. Amen.

Reflection questions:

1. How does your family give to the needy? Do your children participate? How do you decide what to give?

2. Read Matthew 25:34–40, and reflect on the words of Christ. When you think about giving directly to Jesus, how does it change your perspective on giving?

3. Think about what sacrifices your family could make to have more to give to the poor. For instance, would your family be willing to give up sodas for a month to give money to a hunger fund?

"I always told my three children that in life there are two kinds of people: givers and takers. I've always tried to show them to give. In our home, we received everyone. We showed our children to love and respect everyone. Jesus gave us life and we could never give enough."
Marilia Gonzalez, Georgia WMU Language coordinator

And let the peace of God rule in your hearts, to which also you were called in one body; and be thankful.
(Colossians 3:15)

Kitchen Counters

Do you have a catchall space in your house? Maybe it's your couch or your nightstand, but for me, it's my kitchen counter. School papers, mail, diaper bags, car keys, photographs, artwork, and more are scattered from one end of the countertop all the way to the stove. Somewhere in the middle of the mess is a lovely plate rack with my seasonal display, but its beauty is wasted, hidden amidst the clutter.

I have noticed a peculiar pattern in my evenings lately, disturbing enough that I've been doing an investigation. On any given evening, I can be in the cheeriest of moods, when in a matter of moments, I find my insides churning while my face contorts into the image of the meanest mom you've ever met in your nightmares! *What could it be,* I wondered. My first thought (and may I add, my first hope) was that I was having hormonal mood swings. Wouldn't that have been a pleasant answer, letting medication bring a solution! But no, under closer examination of this mystery, I uncovered the truth: I was allowing my temper to flare up because by evening, the clutter on the countertop and the scattering of toys had reached their peaks. I can't stand messiness.

After a brief trip to fantasyland where I entertained the idea of training my family to put everything back where they found it on a consistent basis, I contemplated feeling sorry for myself. *Woe is me; I'm stuck cleaning up after everybody else every night of my life.* But then God stepped into my thoughts. School papers and artwork are on the counter? Those items are there because of the three children I prayed that God would give to me. Car keys? I'm blessed to have reliable transportation for myself and my family. Photographs? Each picture tells a story of a pleasant memory for me. One by one, the pieces of clutter became reminders of God's blessings. And what's more, the little bit of clutter on the counter doesn't matter to

God, but the lives of my husband and precious children playing in the living room are of eternal worth to my heavenly Father.

As you encounter today's clutter and frustrations in your home, ask yourself as a mom and as a child of God: *Does this really matter?* Let your attention rest on what matters most to God—people—then you'll likely find yourself giving each one of them a hug!

Precious Lord, I want to place emphasis on my family more than my house, and on clean hearts more than clean kitchen counters. Where is that line of balance in my home? Help me to find it joyfully. Please clear out the clutter in my heart today. Amen.

Reflection questions:

1. Think about the messiest part of your house that is a constant turnover of clutter. Go to that area and look at each item of clutter as a symbol of life and activity in your home. Spend time thanking God for the blessed lives in your home.

2. Neatness and order in your house is a good goal for everyone to help with, provided your desire for orderliness doesn't overtake your willingness to create a warm and nurturing environment for your children to grow, play, and explore. As you walk through your house, ask God to teach you how to have a home designed for a child's growth, including spiritual, physical, mental, and missional.

3. Relinquish a corner of your house to missions. Designate a space where you and your children can learn about, be reminded of, or do missions. You might include a world map, a bank for a special offering, pictures of people groups, flags, or supplies for an ongoing missions project. Talk with your children about always making room in their lives for serving God, even if it means putting up with a bit of clutter!

"Are you stuck in a rut of regretting the past and fretting about the future? Don't fear that your life will end—fear that it will never begin. So tickle your children until they can stand it no more, laugh until your stomach muscles ache, give hugs freely, cheer loudly when your child is up to bat, sing in the shower, and pray like you've never prayed before."
Brenna Stull, author of Coach Mom: 7 Strategies for Organizing Your Family into an All-Star Team

Who is this King of glory? The L*ORD* *strong and mighty, the* L*ORD* *mighty in battle. The angel of the* L*ORD* *encamps all around those who fear Him, and delivers them.*
(Psalm 24:8; 34:7)

Not China

Do you spend time praying for missionaries with your children? One night, Julia and I were naming different countries of the world, and talking about how we could pray for the missionaries who live there. "Julia, did you know that in China, missionaries face great danger by giving away Bibles?" I asked.

"Oh, no! If the people don't have Bibles, how will they know about Jesus?"

"The missionaries do their best to tell people about Jesus, and they do give away Bibles, but sometimes missionaries and other Christians are put in jail."

"Well, Momma, then who will tell the people about Jesus?"

I looked deeply into those beautiful, innocent brown eyes, and I breathed a quick prayer. "Baby, maybe God will one day send me to China. Or maybe God will ask you to go." Julia had always been excited about the prospect of becoming a missionary, and she was very pleased whenever I had gone on mission trips, but this new piece of information rocked her world; being a missionary could be dangerous.

Julia thought for a few moments, then she spoke. "If God wants me to be a missionary, I will do it. I just hope He doesn't ask me to go to China, and please, don't you ever go to China, Momma."

As I shut her bedroom door, her final words rolled around in my mind, creating giant swells of emotion. I had often prayed for God to use my children in ministry and missions if it would be His will. But in my mind, I had always pictured each of them happy and healthy, fruitful and thriving, and never in chains. *God, please not China*, I prayed. I immediately realized I had prayed a selfish prayer. Is it OK for other people's children to be sent as missionaries to China, just not my children? Can I accept that other Christians suffer for the cause of Christ, as long as it's not my family? Knowing that millions of people around the world are hopeless and oppressed without Christ, can I rest well as long as my God-fearing children are safely tucked in bed each night? And how peculiar that I myself would suffer for Christ much more willingly than I would allow my children to pick up their crosses and follow Christ into danger.

Since that night of prayer with Julia, she often remembers to pray for the people of China. When the country is mentioned on the news, her ears perk up and she wants to know the latest. She continues to pray that our president can talk to the president of China, and that he would invite Jesus into his heart. I see all the signs that for at least this season of my daughter's life, God has given her a burden for the people of this country with such an oppressive government. How shall I respond? How should any kingdom-minded mother respond?

Do you realize the power of your influence over your children? We've probably all been guilty of persuading their young minds to go with the preferences we want them to have, but in no way do we want to interfere with God's calling on their lives for our own selfish desires. Instead, we prepare them to go, we help to build their faith in the King who is mighty to save, we guide them in hearing God's voice, and then we watch and pray. We can be sure God will call our children to minister in His name, whether it's across the street or all the way to China.

Heavenly Father, I stand in awe that You have had a plan for my children's lives before they were even born—before I was even born! Because You know their future and I do not, please lead me as I train them for their future roles in Your kingdom. When I have a selfish motive, whether prideful or possessive of my children, please remind me that they first belong to You. Amen.

Reflection questions:

1. What were your dreams as a child? How did your parents influence your career choices as you grew older?

2. Do you have notions of what your child will do for the kingdom of God? Write these thoughts down, then release each one of them to God. Acknowledge His sovereignty in your child's life.

3. Help your child to memorize 2 Samuel 22:2, and apply the verse whenever a stressful situation arises in your family. Feeling anxious for your child's future? Pray 2 Timothy 4:18 over him.

"If God has called you to be a missionary, don't stoop to be a king."
Charles Spurgeon, renowned preacher of the 1800s

He who walks with wise men will be wise.
(Proverbs 13:20)

One Single Blade of Grass

My son is an explorer. At seven months old he finally was able to crawl—and off he went! He used to enjoy reclining on a blanket beside my desk, passing the time by chewing on toys, but now he's determined to see the world—or at least every square inch of our house. He headed for the kitchen at a snail's pace one day, and then plopped down for just a moment to see if I was watching him. Our eyes met, and his smile invited me to get down on the floor and crawl alongside him. We took off, both of us on all fours, and I realized how looming the world must seem to a little one whose eyes are naturally only about one foot from the floor. Then I saw it: my son had placed his hand upon a small blade of plastic Easter grass, and the green string stuck to his palm. I thanked God for a playful moment that turned into a saving grace, as I was able to find and remove that choking hazard stuck to my son's palm.

It is your privilege as a mother to journey alongside your children as they find Christ and then begin to experience spiritual growth. They will need a gentle nudge from you every once in a while to encourage them to take another step of faith along God's path. Your encouragement and help toward their spiritual growth, whether formal or informal, is discipling. Pray for your children daily, that they might be all that God has called them to be.

Enrich your companionship with your children by adding a fresh dose of compassion. Compassion doesn't require "getting on their level" and joining in with behaviors of spiritual immaturity, but it can mean walking, or crawling, alongside them to gain a glimpse of life from their perspective. Your choice to be a close companion just may reveal to your discerning eyes what your children may be holding on to, unaware of the dangers ahead. A discipling mother who operates out of compassion is a kingdom-minded mother indeed.

Dear Father, help me to be a discipling mother, considering carefully when my children need encouragement. Help me to have the kind of relationship with my children that will allow me to see life from their perspectives, giving me an understanding of their deepest needs. Amen.

Reflection questions:

1. Write down the situations your child will someday face in the future that will be most difficult to understand from his or her perspective.

2. Ephesians 5:1 teaches to "be imitators of God as dear children." Knowing your children will first learn to be an imitator of you, how does this verse challenge you as a mother?

3. What are the marks of discipleship listed in these verses that you can help nurture in your child as he grows in his walk with Christ?

   Matthew 16:24

   John 8:31

   John 15:8

"My children have each told me that the thing they remember most about their childhood is that I was always there to talk with them and listen to their problems. I'm grateful that my children could count on me, and now each moment is a memory."
Alma Osborne, Kimberly's grandmother

"And these words which I command you today shall be in your heart. You shall teach them diligently to your children, and shall talk of them when you sit in your house, when you walk by the way, when you lie down, and when you rise up."
(Deuteronomy 6:6–7)

Up to the Challenge

These words of Scripture can seem like a daunting challenge to any mother. As I read them, the image in my mind is of a mother who is peacefully enjoying pleasant walks with her children; they look into her loving eyes and ask sincere questions about the ways of God. She strokes their soft hair and answers each question with wisdom and care. Then I see her quietly sitting at the kitchen table, snapping pole beans with the help of her calm children, as she tells yet another Bible story with a passion that keeps her children on the edges of their seats. Lastly, my mind's eye sees her tucking those precious babies into bed; each child is squeaky clean, and they willingly obey her request that they get into bed the first time she asks. They reverently bow their heads in prayer before she extinguishes the light beside their beds. I'm not sure who that woman is, but I've never met her, and her life is nothing like mine. And equally important, her children are nothing like mine.

How can we obey the directive given to us in Deuteronomy 6:6–7? Children have a short attention span, and their many needs at any age can seem overwhelming. On top of the speedy feet and swift wit required of any mother simply to keep pace with her children, much of a mother's attention is spent each day on necessary chores—things like tying shoes, packing lunches, scrubbing kitchen floors, and running errands. Perhaps the key to being able to obey this parental directive is in the first sentence: we must have God's words and commandments in our hearts. Life with children can be chaotic and busy, even on a good day. We must devote time each day to study the Word for ourselves as well as to teach it to our children. But for those other hours of the day when we "walk by the way," we're to be diligently teaching God's commandments to our children then too. In a modern context, walking by the way could mean driving back and forth to soccer practice, finger painting in the kitchen, surviving a sleepover with your daughter's friends, or muddling through a "terrible two" day of temper tantrums (thrown by the child, of course!). In these busy, hands-on moments of living with children, we can teach God's statutes to them with what we've implanted in our hearts through Scripture study and memorization. These are the tools for fulfilling Deuteronomy 6:6–7.

With a prepared heart and Holy Spirit help, we moms can be up to the challenge. With God's Word hidden in our hearts, what once seemed like an impossible task is not only doable as a mother, but is an attractive way to spend our days with our children: focused on God in everything we do.

Heavenly Father, Your directive in today's Scripture reading can seem like an impossible task on a busy day. Help me to do first what matters most: spending quiet time alone with You and Your Word. Give me a mind to grasp Your teachings, and implant Your words in my heart. Please bring them to my mind throughout each day, that I might teach them diligently to my children. Amen.

Reflection questions:

1. Meditate on today's Scripture passage. Think about how God's Word is timeless; He meant Deuteronomy 6:6–7 for you, and also for parents who have had varied lifestyles throughout the ages.

2. Are your children accustomed to you interjecting God into your daily conversations? If so, how do they respond?

3. According to Psalm 119:11, what is an important benefit of Scripture memorization? How does that benefit help you to be a kingdom-minded mom?

"Both of our children are doing God's work today. It hasn't always been that way. But whenever they strayed from His ways, His Word came back to their memory. God's Word will not return void. I have always based my teaching on God's Word."
Susan Saleeby, missionary, Niger

For judgment is without mercy to the one who has shown no mercy. Mercy triumphs over judgment.
(James 2:13)

Heads Will Roll!

Heading out the door for vacation with three small children and a truckload (or at least a minivan full) of baby gear is no small feat. Formula was packed, beach toys, diapers—oh! It would never do to leave Bear behind, my son's security sleeping partner. I sent my daughter up the stairs to retrieve Bear so we could hit the road.

Julia was a reluctant helper, but she finally ascended the stairs with a scowl. She bellowed from the top of the stairs, "Here he comes!" She threw Bear over the railing. Bear seemed to float in the air with a slow descent. There was nothing I could do but hold my breath as Bear decided where to land, which happened to be atop a figurine I cherished. The figurine was of a mother holding her infant son, a gift presented to me by dear friends when Jay had arrived home. As Bear collided with the figurine, both tumbled, and the heads of both mother and son were dismembered and rolling on the floor.

Julia was in horror at what Bear had done, but she knew she was to blame. With great panic in her eyes, she scurried to my side and said, "Mommy, I am so sorry." I took in the scene once again, then picked up the headless figurine. Yes, major damage had been done, and the irony was beyond classic; Julia was irritated with her brother and me, and in one throw, she had knocked both of our blocks off.

I was deeply disappointed about the figurine, something I had intended to appreciate for many years to come. My flesh wanted to retaliate against Julia with a stern tongue-lashing. But I thought for a second about why the figurine was precious: it was what it represented, the love of a mother and child, which made the molded piece of clay something to treasure.

I leaned down to Julia as she searched my eyes. "Julia, did you mean to break this?"

"No, Mommy, I didn't, and I am so sorry." (Not just sorry, but *so* sorry.)

"Baby, I forgive you. I wish you hadn't done this, but I know you are sorry, and you are more important to me than the figurine." It was one of those priceless, teachable moments to demonstrate the grace and mercy God has given to us through the blood of Jesus Christ.

Alongside the consequences we sometimes must face because of our poor decisions, God often chooses to apply mercy and grace to our brokenness. If I had punished Julia, I realized it would've likely been as a reactionary payback for what she had taken from me, and not out of a loving desire for her to grow as a person. As you make daily decisions about the role of mercy and grace in disciplining your children, be sensitive to the leading of the Holy Spirit in your heart before you make the choice that heads will roll!

Precious Lord, disciplining children is such a difficult task. I want to know how to teach my child about consequences, while also administering grace and mercy as an example of who You are in my life. Guide me each step of the way, and, Father, guard my hand from disciplining out of revenge. In the Name of Jesus, amen.

Reflection questions:

1. Can you think of a time when you recently punished your child out of revenge? Ask God for forgiveness, and talk with the Lord about how to avoid that parenting pitfall in the future.

2. **What** is the difference between offering mercy in

judgment and excusing poor behavior? How can you express that difference as you interact with your children?

3. Read Matthew 5:44–48 with your children. Even in their youth, God will call upon your children to turn the other cheek to express the grace of God and to create witnessing opportunities. Begin to prepare them to show mercy, and pray together as a family.

"When my children were small, I often heard parents say, 'She's a real mess,' or 'This kid's bad to the bone.' Instead, respect each child and err on the side of mercy. I used to tell my teenage son over and over again, 'Just remember, one day you'll be a godly man.' And today, he is!"
Edna Ellison, author and speaker

"Let the little children come to Me, and do not forbid them; for of such is the kingdom of God."
(Mark 10:14)

On a Cloudy Day

The rain clouds rolled in and my heart began to sink as we drove toward the beach. "Mommy, do you think Alona is already at the beach? I think she is looking for me." My three-year-old Julia was not the least bit concerned about some silly rain spoiling our afternoon by the ocean. After all, we were going to get wet anyway, right? I looked past my windshield and began to pray. Julia and I had made new friends on the beach that morning: a mother, Svletta, and her daughter, Alona. Julia and Alona played well despite the language barrier (Alona was Russian and spoke no English) and Svletta and I agreed to meet back on the beach that afternoon for more playtime. Julia was looking forward to splashing in the waves, and I was counting on an opportunity to witness to Svletta. *Lord, I just know You have given me this opportunity to talk to Svletta about You. Please, God, don't let the rain spoil this opportunity. I have my heart set to share with her!*

With rain clouds looming, two familiar figures came into view. Svletta and Alona were walking on the sidewalk, heading away from the beach. I pulled the car along beside them and rolled down the window. Svletta said she was going home to avoid the storm, and I was in disbelief that my witnessing opportunity was ruined.

Julia and I went ahead on the beach, laughing and playing together in the waves and sand. Suddenly, we spotted a large mass of goop on the beach—a dead jellyfish. She was afraid it would sting her until I blurted out it was dead. I then had to try to explain to my preschooler what it meant to be dead. Oops! "Mommy, what will happen to me when I die?" I looked in the sky and saw powerful rays of sun beginning to burst forth through the gray storm clouds, the very clouds that had caused Julia and I to be alone that afternoon, and I knew I had seen the hand of God. I didn't get to talk with Svletta that day because

God had another appointment for me, an appointment with my own daughter.

Proverbs 16:9 instructs, "A man's heart plans his way, but the Lord directs his steps." God always knows best, doesn't He? God sent in the clouds to clear away any possible distractions so that I might be focused on this special time with Julia, when God would use one of His sea creatures to open a door for me to share the salvation message with her. And with whom besides our children and family could we be more thrilled to have the opportunity to share Christ? I was so determined to share Christ with Svletta, but God's timetable and agenda prevailed. Thank You, God, for the times when You mess up *my* plans to unfold *Your* greater plan in my life.

Heavenly Father, help me not to be so focused on reaching the world for Christ that I neglect the opportunities and the great privilege to share the gospel message with my own children. I am looking with great expectation for the teachable moments You have prepared for me to share Christ with them. Amen.

Reflection questions:

1. How often do you share your faith with people outside of your family? Do you feel comfortable talking about Christ with others? Why or why not?

2. Are you prepared to explain God's plan of salvation to your child when the opportunity arises? Write down God's plan of salvation below. How does John 3:16 explain God's plan to bring the world to a saving knowledge of Jesus Christ?

3. Ask God to make your child's heart soft to the gospel message, and for Scripture to penetrate her heart. Ask the Holy Spirit to convict her of her sins. Pray for godly people to share Christ with your child, and ask for opportunities for yourself to talk about Jesus with her.

"Children are a blessing from God. Parents are responsible for their spiritual and physical growth. Love for God should be revealed through them. The greatest gift they can give their child is guidance down a path that will build moral character complete with Christian values with focus on the kingdom."
Mae B. Williams, Kimberly's grandmother-in-law

Each one should test his own actions. Then he can take pride in himself, without comparing himself to somebody else, for each one should carry his own load.
(Galatians 6:4–5 NIV)

Comparisons

Those Galatians must have had some real issues. According to Paul, they were spending a lot of time looking at what everybody else was doing and judging their works. How terrible! Ummm . . . but that sounds like something that I am sometimes guilty of, and other women I know too. Why do we do that?

The average woman wants to know how she's faring as a mother, as a woman, and as a Christian. Our society tends to endorse a rating system based on comparison. If I'm overweight, that's not so good, but it's OK as long as I'm thinner than my friends! In fact, I can feel rather smug that I'm the smallest and get down right indignant about others' lack of self-control, not noticing my own flaws and weaknesses—and waistline. On the other hand, my weight might be well in hand for my age and body type, but I may beat myself up and try to starve myself if my friends are all pencil-thin. Are you familiar with this mind game? I've played it far too many times, and it's a damaging mind-set for you and your children.

Paul instructs us to examine what we're doing, apart from the work of others. It's a refreshing approach to personal holiness. When I pay attention to others' shortcomings, I can feel critical of them and puffed up about myself. When I try to determine my self-worth by focusing on others' progress, I can feel jealous of them and defeated about myself. Either way, I lose. But when I come into the presence of God and allow Him to examine my life carefully, I will walk away rejoicing. There is great joy in knowing that God is pleased with something happening in my life, and there is great potential for growth when God indicates those areas where I need some Holy Spirit work.

The wisdom of Galatians 6:4–5 has many possible applications for missions-minded moms and their kingdom-hearted kids. Do any of these scenarios seem familiar to you?

1. *"Why can't you be more like your sister?"* When we compare our children to others, we are reinforcing that habit within them. Instead, we can teach them to measure their lives against God's standards.
2. *"But, Mom, all of my friends' moms are letting them do it."* If other parents are making poor choices, they will have to carry that load, but if you make the same bad choice, your load is no lighter because of what all the other moms are carrying!
3. *"How could you behave that way? You are an embarrassment to your father and me."* Making a child believe that his performance is responsible for what others think of his parents is too much pressure and unfair to the child. Ultimately, you want your child to act in a godly manner in order to glorify the Lord, and not because of pride or embarrassment you feel. Who you are as a mom and who he is as a child is wrapped up in Christ, and not in each other, which is good news when it's your kid caught sticking chewing gum on the back of the church pews.

Heavenly Father, I want to evaluate my work privately in Your presence. I desire to know how I can please You alone. Help me to instill within my children that personal connection with You. Amen.

Reflection questions:

1. Are you most tempted to compare yourself to others when it comes to your marriage, child rearing, career, appearance, ministry, or some other area of your life? Is God working in that area of your life, and if so, what exciting movement are you seeing from God? How can comparing yourself to others interfere with what God is doing?

2. No mother wants to do it, but we all have been guilty of comparing our children to others. What would you like to say to your child to affirm what you see that God is doing in her life?

3. Proverbs 14:14 teaches that "a good man will be satisfied from above." Spend time with God today, seeking satisfaction from God in your spiritual life.

"I began by trying to be the perfect combination of June Cleaver, Mother Teresa, and Mary Tyler Moore, but I discovered that God is not so much concerned with the things I do to be the 'perfect mother,' as He is with my willingness to let Him develop in me a 'perfect heart.'"
Martha McMullan Singleton, coauthor of Setting Up Stones: A Parent's Guide to Making Your Home a Place of Worship

Now the LORD was with Jehoshaphat, because he walked in the former ways of his father David.
(2 Chronicles 17:3)

In This Family

Children love to show off, don't they? If a little girl learns to do a cartwheel, be prepared for her to do cartwheels all over the living room for several weeks to come. Little ones who learn to jump will bunny hop until you think you'll go crazy from restraightening the pictures on the wall. And when my son Jay was entering toddlerhood, he was very fond of showing off his impressive ability to scream. If Jay was happy, he'd scream. If something upset him, he'd scream. If he saw an object he liked, or we passed by something he wasn't too fond of, either way he'd scream. We're not talking about a little yelp; we're talking about deafening, screechy, high-pitched screams that could make even the cells in your liver wince. He was loud and constant like a car alarm that couldn't be shut off, and, boy, could he ever do a tap dance on my last nerve.

One day I had the children in the shopping cart as we wheeled through a major department store. Jay was in the front of the buggy, and every sight and sound was giving him cause to scream. People in all directions would stop and stare at us with very unappreciative looks on their faces. I said, "Jay, stop that! We do not scream in this family!" With each screech, the glares worsened, and I continued to scold Jay with an increased volume of my own each time: "Jay! Hush that screaming! We do not scream in this family!" Finally, Jay let out the granddaddy of all screams, and people in three counties turned to stare us down with loathing eyes. I raised my voice to match his screams: "Jay! I told you, WE DO NOT SCREAM IN THIS FAMILY!"

Julia looked at me and said, "But, Momma, you're screaming." Oops.

Do you ever wonder if your children fully grasp the significance and the reality of walking with God? How can you be sure they recognize that Christianity is more than attending church and learning the rules? Your living example before your children will greatly impact their understanding of what it means to live for Christ and to seek first the kingdom of God and His righteousness. As they consider the choices you make when your faith is tested or when serving God becomes trying, they will realize that what you're teaching them about living for God is real, not just words, and that ministry for the Lord is worth the sacrifice.

That day in the store when Julia pointed out that I was not behaving the way our family is to behave, all was not lost. I had to admit that I was wrong to scream, and it was an opportunity to explain why we don't scream in our family—a lovely dish served up with a little bit of humble pie. Setting an example of an authentic walk with Christ doesn't require perfection from mothers, but it does require that we be real. David was not a perfect man, and some of his sins were rather public. However, his walk with God was genuine, and according to Scripture, Jehoshaphat chose to follow in his father's footsteps of faith.

Examine your lifestyle, and ask God to point out any inconsistencies in your behavior versus your beliefs. Little eyes are watching.

Heavenly Father, I want all of who I am and what I do to be under Your authority. I want to be Christlike for Your glory, and for the sake of my children who are learning from my example. Help me to be authentic in my faith. Amen.

Reflection questions:

1. Why doesn't the parenting philosophy of "do what I say and not what I do" work with children?

2. Read Psalm 78:1–8. What are the specific life choices of the fathers listed in verse 8? What would that type of lifestyle look like?

3. Is God speaking to you about any attitudes or actions that you're engaging in that send a mixed message to your children? What are you willing to do about it? What are the possible consequences of willfully continuing in an action that dishonors God?

"Teach by example as well as with words. They will believe what they see more than they will believe what they hear."
Dr. Thelma Wells, president, A Woman of God Ministries; founder of the Ready to Win Conferences; author of Don't Give In—God Wants YOU to Win!

Trust in the LORD *forever, for in YAH, the* LORD*, is everlasting strength.*
(Isaiah 26:4)

Little Red Wagon

The feel of the leather in the little boy's hands thrilled him as he ran his fingers gently over the baseball's red stitching. "Two dollars, Jimmy, and it's yours," said the storeowner. The young boy grinned, then tore out of the front door with excitement. He had an idea.

Early the next morning, Jimmy bundled up in his jacket, mittens, and scarf, and he skipped out of his driveway with an old, rusty red wagon. He passed by garbage cans and stopped at street corners, carefully placing empty glass soda bottles in the wagon. Each clink of the glass nestling in the wagon was as good as a shiny nickel in his pocket. Jimmy thought about the baseball and could almost feel the stitching through his woolen mittens. The sun inched higher in the morning sky, and Jimmy's wagon was heaping full. He stooped to gather one last bottle, and gingerly placed it on top of his load. The bottle teetered dangerously, threatening to topple the entire heap, but then settled into a narrow space. Jimmy straightened his frame and gingerly began to pull his wagon in the direction of the town's glass recycling center. Oh boy! He imagined himself tossing that beautiful white baseball with his daddy in the afternoon sun.

The little town seemed alive with great hustling and bustling that day, and the potholed streets were busy with traffic. A large truck passed near Jimmy, and without warning, the driver honked his horn. The booming sound startled little Jimmy and he jumped, causing the wagon to jolt forward; a pocket full of shiny nickels in the form of empty glass soda bottles came crashing down on the sidewalk. The glass shattered all around the wagon, along with Jimmy's dreams of a game of catch.

The disappointment was more than his young heart could bear, and he sat on the edge of the sidewalk with his face buried in his mittens. Jimmy's tragedy had happened in front of the home of a family friend, Mr. Compole, who came to Jimmy's side as he witnessed what had happened. "Son, what's the matter? Why are you crying, Jimmy?"

"Oh, Mr. Compole, I was collecting bottles to recycle to buy me a new baseball. I've always wanted one, you know." Jimmy's voice began to trail off as he looked back at the scene to recount what had happened. "The truck came by, and my wagon was so full. Everything crashed, and now I've got nothin'." Jimmy looked at Mr. Compole and finished the story with sobs. "I guess my load was just too big."

Mr. Compole wrapped a sympathetic arm around Jimmy's shaking frame. "Jimmy, perhaps it's not that your load was too big. Maybe your wagon was just too small." Mr. Compole and Jimmy swept shards of glass from the cement, and Jimmy managed to smile again when Mr. Compole stepped out of his shed pushing an old, rusty, and very large red wheelbarrow. Jimmy had hope once again.

Children are filled with questions about their futures. What will they grow to be? Whom will they marry? What does God want them to do? You cannot answer any of those questions with any more authority than your children themselves, but you can know that your children will have difficult tasks and challenging troubles to deal with along the way. You can teach them to approach life with a "don't get your wagon too full" mentality, or you can teach them to trust that God is big enough, strong enough, and loving enough to handle all of the challenges they must face.

Just as you have grown in your faith by witnessing God's trustworthiness during challenging moments of your life, your children will learn more about the faithfulness of God by walking through faith-building experiences. Pay attention to God's holy nudges, prompting you to give your children some room to spread their wings spiritually. Kingdom-hearted kids must eventually learn to fully rely on God instead of fully relying on Mom. As your children walk with the Lord, they will learn that it will never be that their load in life is too big, only that in their minds, they've made God too small.

Heavenly Father, please grant me wisdom to know when to let my children take spiritual steps of growth, even when my mother's heart knows that potential difficulty or even heartache are possible outcomes. Amen.

Reflection questions:

1. What experience in your life has taught you the most about God's faithfulness?

2. In what ways have you "made God too small"? Have you minimized God's authority and power to change a situation, or have you doubted His faithfulness?

3. What is the warning in these verses about trust?

Psalm 118:8

Proverbs 3:5

1 Timothy 6:17

"My husband was in the military, and our family moved 22 times. Philippians 4:11 says, 'I have learned, in whatsoever state I am, to be content'—and I had to learn to be content in each of the ten 'states' where we moved! I put my trust in God to take care of my family, and He never failed me. He definitely brought contentment no matter where we were."
Mary Osborne, Kimberly's mother

"Therefore give to Your servant an understanding heart to judge Your people, that I may discern between good and evil. For who is able to judge this great people of Yours?"
(1 Kings 3:9)

She Did It

When your child is potty training, you must have nerves of steel to take her out in public. Any number of scenarios could arise, and none of them come out in a mother's favor. I must have been feeling fearless the day I took potty-training Julia to the department store with me. She's cut from the same cloth as her momma, and we were having a grand time scrutinizing the fashions in the women's department. I stood at one rack, studying the clothing, and Julia stood beside me, checking out the styles at a separate rack, where another woman also stood. Suddenly, as will often occur during the potty-training stage of childhood, an obnoxious odor permeated the air. I had pushed the envelope too far, I was sure of it. I quickly scooped Julia into my arms. I looked at Julia, and Julia looked at me. I looked at the woman, and the woman looked at me. I said, "Julia, baby, did you have a little gas?"

She confidently responded with a booming voice, "No, Mommy. She did it!" As her chubby finger pointed at the woman standing beside me, I felt my face burning and realized I had wasted time applying rouge to my cheeks that morning because I had enough blush on my face to last throughout the day. However, the other shopper . . . well, she did not protest. The toddler with the loud voice and chubby finger must have been telling the truth.

God is a holy and righteous judge, discerning with all wisdom the hearts of man. When Solomon found himself with the task of ruling over a mighty people who were of great worth to the Lord, he sought God's wisdom to judge fairly. Your child is a mighty warrior in training for the Lord, and he is of great worth to the kingdom of God. How will you navigate the many judgments a mother must make in her child's life? You must ask God for wisdom and discernment.

A mother's leadership decisions are many and they are significant. As was the case with Julia in the department store, things aren't always as they appear. The senses can be deceiving, requiring godly discernment. A mother must dig deeper and pray more fervently for the truth. As you seek to make righteous judgments with your children, let them know that you're relying on God for wisdom. Rather than giving the impression that you're always right by motherly instinct, or pridefully rearing up to show your children who's boss, don't be afraid to tell them that you're praying for discernment about their situations. Your willingness to acknowledge that only God has all the answers will encourage your children to turn to God when one day they find themselves searching for answers.

Heavenly Father, I need Your wisdom and guidance to lead my children. I want to be like You, my righteous Judge, but I am so limited to know the truth. God, You see and know all things. Please impart Your wisdom to me, and grant me discernment to know the truth of each matter with my children. I want to be an example to my children, that they will also turn to You for wisdom. Amen.

Reflection questions:

1. What are some of the questions you're currently grappling with as a parent trying to guide your child? Write them below, and pray over each one.

2. When your children come to you for guidance, what can you say that will guide them to the truth while also teaching them to seek God's will? How can you train your children to rely upon God's wisdom instead of the wisdom of a person?

3. What does Hebrews 5:14 teach you about discerning good and evil?

"One day I was sharing with my children that sometimes hearing the same thing repeated through different sources could be God speaking. Several times that day we heard a commercial on TV and the radio about eating broccoli when Ryan said, 'Mama, I think God is trying to tell us to eat more broccoli.'"
Susan Reeves, prayer coordinator, Women's Revival Tour

After these things I looked, and behold, a great multitude which no one could number, of all nations, tribes, peoples, and tongues, standing before the throne and before the Lamb, clothed with white robes, with palm branches in their hands, and crying out with a loud voice, saying, "Salvation belongs to our God who sits on the throne, and to the Lamb!"
(Revelation 7:9–10)

Every Crayon in the Box

Little Julia was coming home each week with beautiful creations made with glue, paint, crayons, glitter, pompoms—you name it! It was her first Christmas of coloring within the lines, and I was proudly displaying each masterpiece on the refrigerator. One day she pulled out her latest creation: a coloring sheet of Baby Jesus in a manger. Julia had given Baby Jesus a brown face. I wondered if perhaps Julia had been given a limited number of crayons to pick from, but then I noticed how the manger was a different and much lighter shade of brown altogether. Puzzled, I asked, "Julia, did you notice that you colored Baby Jesus brown?"

Unshaken, Julia responded proudly, "Yes, Momma. I just wanted to. Isn't He beautiful?"

One of Julia's little brothers is our adopted son, Jay, of Latin descent, so mine is a multicolored family. In fact, Julia has light brown hair, Jay has black hair and darker skin, and our youngest son has blond hair and fair skin. We use up nearly every crayon in the box for our family portrait! As we run errands about town, we sometimes receive sideways glances and the occasional odd comment. Adults are color aware, even those who don't want to carry prejudice in their hearts. As children grow, they seem to be hardwired to pick up cues from adults to learn how to interact with other people in the world.

As the parent, your children watch to see what you embrace and what makes you feel uncomfortable. How will you help to shape their perceptions of different skin colors? The world is filled with people of many different colors, all of whom will be represented around God's throne one day in glory. How you help your children to frame relationships now can have a profound impact on their willingness as adults to reach out to individuals for the kingdom of God.

My children will likely have to deal with prejudiced comments and behaviors all of their lives because of our colorful blend. I don't look forward to the day my babies come home with tear-stained cheeks because of a thoughtless comment made by a child or, just as likely, an adult. However, no family is exempt from facing racial issues head-on. Your children will walk through those same doors of decision, and as a mother desiring to instill a kingdom heart in her children, you will need to have a soul-searching talk with the Lord to help you prepare your children to minister to others in a color-filled world.

Heavenly Father, search my heart and tell me what You see. What are my attitudes about people of other cultures and colors? I want to offer compassion, not pity. I want to love, not tolerate. I want to lift up, not tear down. Be my guide, O Lord, I pray. Amen.

Reflection questions:

1. How often do your children see you interact with people of other cultures? Is your neighborhood multicultural? Your church family? Are your friendships? Your work relationships?

2. Are you aware of any negative perceptions you have about people who are different, from different cultural groups or countries? Write them down. Have you ever experienced stereotyping because of your culture? What were those stereotypes?

3. Meditate on the following verses, allowing the Holy Spirit to give you wisdom as a mother to help mold your child's perceptions of people and cultural groups.

   Acts 10:34–35

   Romans 2:11

   Philippians 2:10–11

"One night my children's devotional focal passage was: 'God said, "Let the earth be filled with animals." Then God said, "Let us make human beings"' (Genesis 1:24, 26 ICB). After a story, I asked my four-year-old, 'What does God do for the animals?' She answered, 'He gives them beans.' Wondering, I asked, 'What kind of beans?' With confidence she said, 'Human beans!'"
Susan F. Blackmon, mother

A word fitly spoken is like apples of gold in settings of silver.
(Proverbs 25:11)

Leaving a Scar

As the doctor pronounced that my son wouldn't need stitches in his head, I was relieved. However, the sensation only lasted a moment, because then he said, "But he'll have a scar." My beautiful baby, plump with baby fat, already had a scar on his young body. His blond hair was stained blood red from the wound he received from his fall, but the blood would wash away. The scar would last a lifetime.

Words can have the same effect. Hurtful words create a wound that can be cleaned up with apologies and healed with love and forgiveness, but they can still leave a scar. Though I've forgiven people who have said unkind words to me in the past, I can still remember the exact words they said to bring injury to me, much more clearly than I remember their words of apology. When I reflect on those unkind words directed toward me a year ago or perhaps even ten years ago, I can still feel the pain. The wound is healed, but the scar remains.

Does your heart bear any scars from hurtful words? Perhaps a teacher, a friend, a coach, a man, or even a parent said words that made you feel empty and worthless, dumb, clumsy, unattractive, or ashamed. The sad truth is that as much as we despise the way others have injured us with words, we are no less able to control our tongues to keep from hurting others in the same way. The Bible calls the tongue untamable, "an unruly evil, full of deadly poison" (James 3:8).

Words spoken by loved ones are especially significant, because we highly value what they think of us. As a mother, your children take your words of evaluation seriously. Your children may conceal their interest in your opinions, but the applause of a mother is the most important sound in the audience to any child on the stage. The challenge every mom faces is how to offer constructive criticism to help her child improve and grow, while not crushing the spirit of the child.

God's solution? A word fitly spoken. The apples described in Proverbs 25:11 are pleasing to the eye and sweet to taste. Words that roll off the tongue in haste or in anger will be ragged and stained, but what is said with forethought and care will be refined as gold, and sparkling like silver. Your child will be beaten down with critical words throughout his lifetime, but he will cherish the words of encouragement and blessing you have given to him.

Evaluate your communication with your child today. If you're like me, some days lend themselves to words of praise more than others. During those times when I find myself correcting one of my little ones throughout the day, I hunt carefully to catch him doing something good, giving me an opportunity to affirm him for what he is doing well. With God's help, even words of correction can be words fitly spoken, which will never leave a scar.

Heavenly Father, I want my communication with my child to be wholesome and encouraging. Please make me more aware of my words today, thinking before I speak, to offer words that are fitly spoken. Amen.

Reflection questions:

1. Jesus is our perfect example in all things, including communication. Think about Jesus' conversation with the woman who was caught in adultery (John 8:1–12), or with the woman at the well (John 4). What was Jesus' way of communicating correction without crushing either woman's spirit?

2. What is the danger of saying only words of praise and never words of correction to your children?

3. Read James 3:1–12, describing our plight with taming our tongues. Ask God to convict you of any changes you need to make in your communication with others, including your children.

"Disciplining our children in a consistent, calm, assertive, and loving manner is very important. We remember not to punish our little ones with words that tear down their confidence; it's vital for their lives to be healthy—mentally and emotionally—so they can best fulfill God's special plan for them."
Debra W. Sowell, Kimberly's mother-in-law

Remember now your Creator in the days of your youth, before the difficult days come, and the years draw near when you say, "I have no pleasure in them."
(Ecclesiastes 12:1)

Precious Memories

It's always fun when my two older sisters and brother and I get together and begin sauntering down memory lane. As we giggle about funny tricks we pulled on Mom and Dad or reminisce about favorite family vacations, our minds seem to be in unison. However, it's amazing how none of us can agree on certain other memories. Each of us recalls a little differently who always got the last piece of cake, who got away with the most mischief, who had to wear the ugliest hand-me-down outfits, or who did the most chores. Once the four of us begin to disagree, the ball starts rolling downhill, and we remember more things differently than we do the same.

The measuring stick mothers often use to evaluate themselves is the number of and quality of the experiences they give to their children. Do you ever think about what memories your children will take with them into adulthood? We assume that fun moments will instantly transform into fond memories, but most of those memories will eventually blur and fade together, creating one blanket of pleasant oblivion. If you'll think back into your own childhood, certainly a few special memories pop up, like a special Christmas program or a particular birthday party, but the vast majority of your childhood moments are gone from your memory. Countless hours of your life are tucked deeply into your brain, never to be retrieved. Your childhood memories are best described as either a shade of light or a curtain of darkness from your past.

What do you want your children to remember from their childhoods? What consumes most of your resources as a mother? The writer of Ecclesiastes teaches that a moment will come for your children in their adult lives when they will find no pleasure in that day. Your children won't be able to fall back on memories of pony rides or vacations for comfort. Expensive toys or elaborate birthday parties won't give them hope in the darkness of night. These are the days that you have also experienced, when you could not see God with your physical eyes so you were thankful you'd been trained to see Him with your spiritual eyes, to reach out and lay hold of Him because you instinctively knew He was there.

In their youth, children need to be building a solid understanding of God—His nature, His ways, His faithfulness, His instruction—in preparation for the challenges of adulthood. To "remember" can also be translated as "recall" or "retrieve." As adults, your children will only be able to retrieve what has been implanted into their childhoods. Specific memories fade, yes, but wisdom of the heart is a treasure your children will draw upon for a lifetime.

Dear Lord, help me to evaluate my decisions as a mother and the experiences that I give to my children. Teach me to place the emphasis of their childhood on knowing Christ and living for Him. Amen.

Reflection questions:

1. Think for a few moments about your favorite childhood memories. How many can you name? If each of those specific memories represented one day of your life, how many days of your childhood can you not remember?

2. Did you grow up in a home where you were taught knowledge of God? How did your upbringing and exposure to God as a child affect your approach to trials as an adult?

3. Imparting a knowledge of God to your children may not seem as glamorous as hosting the best birthday parties on the block. What are the pressures you face as a mother to keep up with other families' expectations? Apply Proverbs 14:12 to your approach to motherhood, resolving to be the mom God has called you to be.

"God will only be as real to your children as He is in your own life. Let your kids see you read your Bible and pray. Talk about what He is doing in your life. Keep His name on your lips. Genuine faith is contagious; they will catch it."
Christie Seeley, missionary

"For there is born to you this day in the city of David a Savior, who is Christ the Lord."
(Luke 2:11)

First on the List

As we sat in the drive-through line just days before Thanksgiving, my mind began to wander to the day *after* Thanksgiving: that busiest of days for women all over America, the biggest shopping day of the year. I had most of my Christmas shopping already completed, but how can the mother of any four-year-old ever truly know what her child wants for Christmas? Since early January, Julia had been telling me about all of the things she wanted to put on her Christmas list, from dolls and princess gowns to ant farms and drum sets. A trip to the toy store or browsing through a toy catalog only exasperated the riddle of what to get this child, as Julia had me cross-eyed from her quick and vigorous finger-pointing coupled with chants of: "Mommy, I want that, and that, and that, and that, and that, and . . ." What, oh, what, is a mother to do?

I had asked Julia several times to tell me what she wanted to ask for, but every time I knew I was getting a four-year-old response. "Mommy, I want a trampoline." Oh, really? Never before had she shown interest in a trampoline until someone in her Sunday School class wanted one. I was already educated about that monkey-see, monkey-do act Julia had learned, and she played that game frequently. How could I pose the question to Julia in such a way as to unlock the mystery of what she most desired in her heart? I finally formulated the perfect question. "Julia, Mommy really wants to know what you want for Christmas. If you could only have one thing for Christmas and that's all, what would be that one thing that you want with all your heart?"

A sweet voice from a little girl with bright eyes immediately responded, "Jesus." As a quick, off-the-cuff response, somehow I knew that what she said was true. I immediately had to tell God that what I most wanted for

Christmas was what had just come out of my daughter's mouth—a child who longs for the Savior.

What are you longing for with all your heart? If Jesus is on the top of your list, you will not be disappointed. The angel told the shepherds, "Unto you." Jesus is a gift God has given directly to you. Rejoice! Your desire to raise children with a passionate longing for Jesus Christ will be fulfilled as you teach them about the many benefits of the Savior, and as you exhibit that great longing for Christ in your own life. Monkey-see, monkey-do? Your choice to put Jesus first doesn't guarantee that He'll be their top priority, but your genuine hunger and thirst for God will lead your children to further explore what's so wonderful about Jesus. And as they learn about His ways for themselves, you can believe that one day the name of Jesus will be at the top of their lists.

Heavenly Father, I want my heart's longings to align with what You have offered to me: a Savior, Christ the Lord. Teach my heart to long for Jesus more than any worldly trinket, and I pray the same for my children. Amen.

Reflection questions:

1. Based on your actions and attitudes, would your children guess that Jesus is your greatest desire? Why or why not?

2. How can you combat materialism in your family to help your children value spiritual blessings more than "stuff"?

3. Read Matthew 6:33. Share this verse with your children, and pray as a family about how to put God first in your lives.

"The presence of wealth is no protection against the ravages of the soul. Emptiness still stalks the rich, loneliness still haunts the icon, and disappointment still casts its shadow amidst the cheers under the spotlight."
Ravi Zacharias, author of Recapture the Wonder

"I do not pray that You should take them out of the world, but that You should keep them from the evil one. They are not of the world, just as I am not of the world. Sanctify them by Your truth. Your word is truth. As You sent Me into the world, I also have sent them into the world."
(John 17:15–19)

In the World

I suppose every elementary school classroom has one rowdy little boy that demands an extra helping of time and attention, and my daughter's kindergarten class was no exception. We'll call him Thomas, and he was quite a rounder. Julia came home telling stories about him during the first week of school. She wasn't afraid of Thomas, but he seemed to command a large audience with his misbehavior.

One day I visited Julia's classroom for a special activity, and I was glad to finally meet the infamous Thomas. I noticed right away that his desk was rather close to Julia's. I introduced myself, and the two of us began to talk. I remarked how big and strong he was, and how he could use his muscles to be a big helper to his teacher, but a student sitting nearby piped up, "No, not Thomas. He never helps. He just gets in trouble all the time."

I made a second attempt, telling Thomas how his smile was bright and pleasant, making him look friendly. Immediately another child spoke, "Not Thomas. He's mean to everybody. Our class never gets tokens because he messes it up all the time." Another little voice remarked that she was afraid of Thomas, and then another. I finally shut my mouth.

That night, Julia and I talked about how she could be a friend to Thomas. We talked about how Thomas must've felt when everyone was saying negative things about him at lunch, and Julia began to see the situation from his point of view. We resolved to pray for him at least once a day, and Julia decided to continue to try to play with him and say encouraging words to him. My heart was filled with warm fuzzies as I thought about my baby befriending a hurting child.

A few weeks into Operation Pray for Thomas, I learned that Thomas had injured another little girl at school in a rather cruel and unfeeling way. My mind raced through a series of possible scenarios. Would Julia be next? In an effort to be encouraging, would she one day go too far, or would she be his next victim because she caught Thomas in a bad mood? I immediately wanted to transform Operation Pray for Thomas into Operation Stay Ten Feet Away from Thomas!

I began searching for some answers to questions I didn't want to have to ask. Does the mandate to "be in the world but not of the world" apply to children? How far "in" should a five-year-old be expected to go? Could she make a difference in a confused little boy's life? And what about Thomas? If not one classmate would befriend him, how would that affect his young life? I thought about my baby, and I thought about Thomas. My mind turned to Thomas's mother and the emotions she must've been experiencing.

Children have the ability to influence others for Christ. The more I thought about Jesus' prayer to the Father (John 17:15–19), I realized that I don't have a choice—my children will be in the world whether I like it or not. That's where we live! My children can't impact the world for Jesus if I barricade them from anyone who isn't Christian. As they interact with those who don't know Christ, they will learn to recognize the needs of the lost, and God will begin to develop in them a passion for the lost. My responsibility as a mother is to teach my children to be wise in their interactions with others, to help strengthen them to reject worldly temptations, and to know when to pull back the reins when I sense they're delving into territory they aren't spiritually equipped yet to handle. Following the example of Jesus, I can pray for God to protect them from the evil one, and I can pray for God's truth to sanctify their hearts.

Phew! That's no cookie-cutter answer to the tough questions kingdom-minded moms must ask, but with God's help, our children can thrive as salt and light in this world where Jesus has sent us.

Heavenly Father, I want my children to impact their corners of the world for Christ. Please guide them to interact wisely with lost people around them, and help me distinguish where to draw healthy boundaries for them based on discernment and not fear. Amen.

Reflection questions:

1. Have you experienced internal struggles about safeguarding your child while he is "in the world"?

2. Do you know any children like Thomas? What is your approach to how your child will interact with the Thomases of the world? Would that approach differ between the different children in your family?

3. Meditate on John 17:15–19. Jesus has sent you into the world. Look around at the people in your community of life. Have you embraced God's call to be in the world for His mission?

"A couple of years ago, my youngest daughter decided to do missions in Senegal. Imagine my surprise when she traveled to the same location where I had done missions seven years before, even working with some of the same missionaries. God reassured me that He had worked in the hearts of my children, even before I could see it."
Tricia Scribner, author and apologist

Then the mother of Zebedee's sons came to Him with her sons, kneeling down and asking something from Him. And He said to her, "What do you wish?" She said to Him, "Grant that these two sons of mine may sit, one on Your right hand and the other on the left, in Your kingdom."
(Matthew 20:20–21)

Me First

Kids always want to be first. They push to get the first sip at the water fountain. They want to be first down the slide. My children fuss to get the first slice of cake or to be first to kiss their daddy hello in the evenings. All of this pushiness and selfish behavior—how rude! But sometimes we mommies can get pushy too.

Mothers love their children and see the potential for their greatness. When I coached high school softball, the parents often kept me on my toes because they wanted their daughters to have the first opportunity to perform and achieve. I tried to relate to their concerns, but it wasn't until I was a mother sitting in the stands while my daughter was skipped over in the batting rotation during a T-ball game that I understood that powerful emotion that wells up when a mother senses her child being shortchanged. The emotion can sweep over us without any warning, whether it's about sports teams, spelling bees, prom dates, church choir solos, accelerated classes at school, or even long lines at the amusement park. If we're going to teach our children to put others first, we've got to learn to be at peace when other people begin piling up before our child in line.

The mother of James and John had lofty ambitions for her sons. She sensed great leadership potential in her two boys, and she came to Jesus along with James and John, hoping to secure the promise that they would be pushed to the head of the line when Jesus began passing down honors and positions. Little did she or her sons realize that their future moments of glory would have nothing to do with cushy positions of authority and leisure, and everything to do with hardship and self-sacrifice. What motivated the mother of James and John to talk to Jesus on their behalf? After all, if she believed her sons to be the best choices for leadership in Jesus' kingdom, shouldn't such mighty men be able to talk with Jesus about holding rank without their mother having to intervene? I have often wondered if she was driven by her own pride to push for their promotion. No mom enjoys watching her child sit on the bench, and the mother of James and John didn't want to watch other men enjoying power and position instead of her own sons.

Jesus said, "'If anyone desires to be first, he shall be last of all and servant of all'" (Mark 9:35). Paul taught, "Let nothing be done through selfish ambition or conceit, but in lowliness of mind let each esteem others better than himself" (Philippians 2:3). These principles look good on paper and we easily agree to teach them to our children, but how we react when our children aren't placed on the top of the list will teach more to them than what we say in theory. Take heart and remember, there's great value in a child learning to be second, or third, or even passed over, as preparation for putting others first for the cause of the gospel.

Heavenly Father, I want my children to do well in life, but I also realize the importance of putting others first as a witness to reach people for Christ. Thank You for the beautiful example of Jesus, who laid aside His glory to meet our need for a Savior. Help me to teach my children to be humble and to accept the call to put others before themselves. Amen.

Reflection questions:

1. Do any of your children tend to be selected for special honors, or often passed over for opportunities? How have you responded?

2. How can you explain to your child the importance of putting others first so that she understands the impact on the kingdom of God? How would you distinguish for your child the difference between being a humble servant and being a doormat?

3. Read the following verses for words of encouragement to those who put others first.

   Isaiah 66:2

   John 13:12–15

   James 4:10

"I have friends who know many families living overseas as missionaries. They have pictures of them, and each night at dinner they pray for one of them. They get prayer letters from the missionaries and can share with the family what is happening. Now, when I am in the States and go visit, the children know me."
Karen, serving in Europe

Be anxious for nothing, but in everything by prayer and supplication, with thanksgiving, let your requests be made known to God; and the peace of God, which surpasses all understanding, will guard your hearts and minds through Christ Jesus.
(Philippians 4:6–7)

All You Can Do

I was resting in my bed staring at the ceiling and evaluating my recent life choices. I was a teenage girl with a bright mind and a lot of opportunities, but I felt fairly confident that I would one day live in poverty as a used and neglected woman as a result of the life path I had already begun to travel. I didn't relish the idea of having a life of turmoil, but I wasn't sure how to turn myself around with such a crowded party of rowdy companions wandering with me on the road to destruction. Doomed, hopeless, and numb was how I felt in the darkness of my bedroom. But then I heard their voices.

Just a few steps down the hallway from me were my parents, talking in hushed tones in their bedroom. My mother's voice was breaking up in soft sobs, and she and my father talked back and forth in short sentences. I inched closer to my bedroom door, trying to catch their words, wondering how much they knew about my secrets and deceptions I was working so hard to conceal from them. They didn't know details, but they knew enough. Then their tone changed; they weren't talking to each other anymore. They were talking to God, lifting my name up in prayer. They cried out to the heavenly Father to do what they could not—heal my darkened soul. As I crouched on my bedroom floor and listened to what they were saying about me to the Father, my face was stained with tears. I could only bear to listen a short while, and then I dragged my hardened heart back into bed. I did not repent of my ways that night, but it marked the beginning of the end of a destructive pattern in my life that had effectively threatened to steal my future from me.

Several years passed before I could talk to my mother about what had happened as the sounds of her whispered prayers passed several feet down the hallway into my troubled ears that night. I wanted to know what she remembered of that event that had been so pivotal in my change of heart. I wanted her to tell me what she was thinking, and how she was feeling. I wondered how those prayers affected her own soul. My mother explained to me, "We knew we couldn't fix what was going on in your life. There comes a time when you can't make the decisions for your children, and all you can do is pray. That's what we did. Then we turned it over to the good Lord to take care of you—and He did!"

Each stage of your child's growth promises to give you reminders that ultimately you are not in control of her life—God is. When your child is sick beyond medicine, or is keeping secrets from you, or is wavering with decisions you cannot make for her, you come face to face with your personal limitations as a mother. But praise be to God, what a comfort to know that the God of the universe, the Almighty One who is everywhere at all times, knowing all, able to do all things, always faithful and true, is the One on the throne. As you learn to rely on God for His care for your child, make sure she also is fully aware of God's authority in her life, that she might turn to Him for guidance and strength.

Precious mother and sister in Christ, don't wait until you feel hopelessly out of control. In all things and at all times, lift up your child's name in prayer.

Heavenly Father, You know everything and have the power to transform and shape my child's life in a way that I cannot. Teach me to turn to You in all things concerning her life. I welcome Your peace in my heart. Amen.

Reflection questions:

1. If your children are older, have you already faced trying times with the strong will of a child? If your children are younger, what are some of the issues you anticipate having to face with them?

2. Have you ever felt out of control of a situation as a mother? What did you do?

3. How do these verses instruct you about your prayers?
   Colossians 4:2

   1 Thessalonians 5:17

   1 Timothy 2:8

"When the time came to tell our children about a new position offered to my husband in a church far away, our older son appeared to know what was about to be said. When we asked, my son replied that he knew we would be moving. God answered our prayers by preparing his heart to accept what God had planned next for our family."
Janet Natale, mother

The whole body, joined and knit together by what every joint supplies, according to the effective working by which every part does its share, causes growth of the body for the edifying of itself in love.
(Ephesians 4:16)

Scaredy-Cat

I'm such a daredevil. I love to take risks, within reason, of course, and I greatly admire others who do so. I highly value a confident and courageous spirit, and I was ecstatic to see that same spirit in my daughter. She'll try any activity, talk to anyone, get on a stage in a heartbeat (good luck getting her off the stage!), sing in public, and ride only the most thrilling rides at the fair. That's my girl! I see the same boldness in my third child, and it thrills my soul. He's a chip off this ole block. But Jay . . . well, he sometimes whimpered at the sight of his shadow. Even as a three-year-old, he screamed and cried throughout every haircut, hid behind my legs when strangers said hello, and refused to ride even most kiddie rides. I struggled to know how to react because his fearful attitude was foreign to me.

One day we were at a restaurant geared toward young children, and a costumed character was greeting families throughout the dining room. As soon as Jay laid eyes on the character, he began to panic, and ear-piercing shrieks of terror were exploding from his lungs. No amount of coaxing or reasoning would change his mind—he wanted that character nowhere near him. Though I was embarrassed because of the scene he caused, I realized that I actually felt angry with him for being afraid. I had tried to shame him into befriending the character, pointing out that his older sister and even his baby brother were talking with him. *Why is he such a scaredy-cat? Why can't he be more like . . . me?*

In the body of Christ, we all have different gifts and talents. As a result, we have different likes and dislikes, and we value different things. I value adventure, while a cautious person like Jay values safety. I want to plunge in and look around, while others may want to look around several times before deciding to take a plunge. Who's right? Neither approach makes a Christian better equipped than the other to serve the Lord in the kingdom of God, but the cautious and the adventurous will likely serve in different capacities. What we must learn to do is appreciate the strengths, gifts, and approaches of others in the body of Christ, realizing that everyone has something to contribute.

Likewise, we as mothers must learn to appreciate the many nuances of our children, knowing that God has knitted each person a bit differently from his earliest days in the womb. God doesn't call upon a mother to make her children into cookie-cutter versions of herself; instead, a kingdom-minded mother will help her children to develop their strengths and gifts, learning to do their share for the kingdom of God.

Who knows? Perhaps Jay's cautious spirit will one day keep me from making a dangerous plunge. Or maybe one day my adventurous spirit will talk Jay into riding a roller coaster. Nah.

Heavenly Father, thank You for the gifts and abilities You have given my children, and for their wonderful personalities. Knowing they are made in Your image, they are precious and of great worth to me and to the kingdom of God. Help me to recognize and nurture all of the wonderful traits You have poured into their lives. Amen.

Reflection questions:

1. In what ways are your children different from you? In what ways are they similar? Do they carry any similar traits to you that you wish they didn't have?

2. What special gifts and characteristics have you noticed in your children that are gifts from God to serve in His kingdom?

3. Spend time praying for your children to find their roles in the family of God, using their gifts to build up the body of Christ in love.

"Conner and Courtney are both sensitive to missions, but their approach is totally different. Conner chose to backpack across Jordan and stay in Bedouin tents, but Courtney chose sports ministry and singing at women's conferences in Armenia. I love how God uses their different personalities and gifts to bring glory to Himself."
Kelly King, Women's Missions and Ministries Specialist, Baptist General Convention of Oklahoma

"And a little child shall lead them."
(Isaiah 11:6)

One Hundred Invitations

"Mommy, I want to invite everyone in my class at school to come to high attendance day at church."

"Sure, baby. I'll be glad to help with the invitations."

"Mommy, I want to invite everyone in the whole kindergarten. They need to learn about Jesus. I even want to invite all of the teachers and their helpers, the art teacher, music teacher, librarians, and the principals!"

By now I was mentally tallying how many invitations my five-year-old and I would be decorating, but Julia still wasn't done. "And you know I can't forget about all of the children in my gymnastics class and on my soccer team. Can we invite them and their families?"

"Sure, baby, why not? You're right—we need to invite everyone to come to church to learn about Jesus." And 100 invitations later, Julia had invited everyone in her sphere of influence to come to church with her.

As high attendance day neared, my husband and I listened to Julia chatter excitedly about how crowded her Sunday School room would be. She was giddy with excitement, wondering how her teacher would fit all of those chairs into one room. Kevin and I exchanged nervous glances. Should we go ahead and break the news to her that 100 families wouldn't be filing into her room on Sunday? Then I was convicted of my tiny faith and cynical attitude. Should I be surprised if God nudged 100 families to follow my five-year-old to Sunday School? And how many people in my sphere of influence had I invited? A select number, but it fell quite short of 100. We prayed with Julia that God would use those invitations as He desired to get people interested in Jesus, and we looked forward to high attendance day.

In a world filled with critics and skeptics, have we allowed the world's cynicism to creep into our own hearts? Have we lost faith that people are still seeking and finding

God? Julia has childlike faith in great measure, the kind of faith that expects results because God reigns on high. Her heart isn't tainted by rejections and disappointments, but then again, God has never rejected me or disappointed me, and my faith is in God and not man, so . . . can I not also have childlike faith in great measure?

Sometimes raising kingdom-hearted kids is less about what we teach our children and more about not squelching what God is doing in their hearts. Do you need a healthy dose of childlike faith? Delve into your heart and examine your faith. It's time for the people of God to start believing once again in the power of God, and acting boldly with great hope. Jesus still saves! Work alongside your children to invite people to church, and let's invite them to meet the Savior, Jesus Christ.

Father, I know You are calling all people to Yourself, but hearts of men seem so cold. Help me to have childlike faith that expects to see God-sized results, propelling my children and me into the world to invite people to meet Jesus. I pray in the name of Jesus, my Savior. Amen.

Reflection questions:

1. When opportunities arise to invite people to church or to talk with them about God, how often do you include your children in the process? What are the benefits of allowing your children to see your example? What are the benefits of allowing your children to take the lead?

2. Having a kingdom heart means seeing God at work in every situation, then being the hands and feet of Christ as He leads. Does your child have a concern about a problem in your community, in the world, or in a family you know? Talk with your child about what he can do to bring the love and truth of Christ into that situation. Be prepared to make personal sacrifices yourself to help your child fulfill what God lays upon his heart.

3. Read Romans 15:4. What Scriptures can you teach to your children to build their hope in Jesus Christ as the Savior of the world?

"When my children didn't feel well, I would lay my hands on that hurting area and pray for God to heal them. Once when I was sick, my five-year-old daughter said, 'Mommy, let me lay my hands on you and pray for you to feel better.' How awesome to know that a child can know the healing power of prayer."
Marie Alston, author, speaker, and vocalist

By this we know love, because He laid down His life for us. And we also ought to lay down our lives for the brethren.
(1 John 3:16)

For the Sake of the Son

Every job has its hazards, and one of the great dangers that comes along with mothering is the terrible temptation to feel overworked and underappreciated. Can you relate to the mother in this poem?

'Twas the night before Christmas and all through the
house
The mommy was calling her husband a louse.
Her children and husband had all gone to bed,
Not noticing the mother wore a crazed look of
dread.
There were toys to assemble and presents to wrap
"You can do it," said Daddy. "For you it's a snap."
Oh, yes, it's a snap, as was addressing each Christmas
card,
Baking dozens of cookies, and stringing lights in the
yard.
Not to mention finding a gift for his crazy Aunt
Mandy,
And chasing wild children hyped up with Christmas
candy.
When what to the mommy's weary eyes should
appear,
But the ink-filled pages of the calendar from this
year.
Oh, the day trips, how fun, and the family nights,
how merry,
And the warm summer days filled with peanut
butter and jelly.
Then her eyes filled with tears as she looked to the
mantle
At a Nativity scene and a barn filled with cattle.
How inconvenient for Mary to give birth in a stable,
When God in His glory was perfectly able
To send forth His Son in finery and show,

Yet Jesus came forth very humbly and low.
"Oh, it's not about me," the mother now mused,
As her thoughts now assembled from what was confused.
"Mary was humbled for the sake of her Son,
And I will be humble for my children, each one."
She gingerly stroked every stocking with care,
Thanking her God for the names stitched on there.
As she finished with presents and pulled her covers up tight,
She rejoiced with great joy and slept soundly that night.

Mary, the mother of Jesus, is a wonderful example to teach us the significance of humble service as mothers. Was God trying to prove something to Mary by having her give birth in a stable? Perhaps, we can't know for sure, but the more obvious reason for these humble birthing circumstances was for the Son of God to enter the world as one meek and poor, a Savior for all men. Simply put, the circumstances were not so much about the mother as they were for the sake of the Son. Time and time again, Mary was forced into trying or uncomfortable circumstances because of God's plan unfolding in her Son's life, yet the fruitfulness of the life of Christ on this earth surely filled every void in Mary's heart with a great joy and satisfaction that only a mother could appreciate.

You, too, are often called upon by God to endure humbling moments of service, often without thanks, for the sake of your children. When you're called to be a mother, much of your life's tasks are not about you; sometimes your children's life lessons will be woven into the fabric of your life. As you find yourself facing new problems today because of your children's situations, or completing some menial task well beneath your abilities for the sake of your family, take heart that your labors are not in vain. God is developing a kingdom heart in your children, and you are God's servant in completing His will for those young lives you tuck into bed each night.

As Christ sacrificed His own life for you, be willing to live sacrificially for the spiritual growth of your children.

Dear Father, thank You for the reminder that my life is not about me. First and foremost, my life is about pleasing You and doing Your will, and I know that part of fulfilling that role is to serve my family with the humble tasks of motherhood. I want to embrace my humble service with a grateful heart to glorify You and bless my children. Amen.

Reflection questions:

1. According to Jesus' words in Matthew 20:28, why did Jesus come? Apply the Lord's description of His life's purpose to God's purpose for you as a mother. Write your thoughts below.

2. There's no doubt about it, some of your labors of love for your children will go without thanks from them. Pray for your children, that they will be willing to serve God all the days of their lives in quiet shadows without the notice of man's eyes, all for the glory of God.

3. How does Christ's example described in the following verses inspire you to serve your family with a humble heart?

John 13:14

2 Corinthians 8:9

Philippians 2:7

I want to run this race with patience
And some day sit down at His feet
When all my earthly cares forgotten
When my journey home has been complete.
Delphia O'Dell, Kimberly's grandmother

Author's Note: My Grandma O'Dell passed away many years ago, but the memory of her selfless love lives on today. She was a caregiver for many years to my grandfather, yet she still sought ways to serve others as an expression of love. These words from a song she wrote reveals her source of hope and strength.

The hearing ear and the seeing eye, the L*ORD* *has made them both.*
(Proverbs 20:12)

Get in the Car

"Hurry up! Get in the car! We need to get home." It was Wednesday night after church, and I was anxious to get home before dark. I clicked the unlock button on my car remote as we rushed toward the vehicle, trying to speed up the process. My daughter couldn't move fast enough to suit me, and I couldn't *believe* she wanted to play pretend games when she knew I was in such a hurry.

"But, Mommy, this isn't our car." She hesitated at the back door of the vehicle as if she was afraid to get in, so I yanked open the back door. "Mommy! This isn't our car! There's no place for me to step up!" She pointed where a running board would be.

"Of course this is our car. Get in!" I impatiently picked her up and hoisted her into the car seat. It wasn't her car seat. It wasn't my car. Someone else at church with a vehicle very similar in appearance to mine had parked near me and left the doors unlocked. I'm not sure if I was more embarrassed because I had to take my child out of someone else's car and gently shut the back door, or because my preschooler was right and I was wrong.

Rush, rush, rush—it's a common way of life for moms. Whether I'm multitasking with laundry, dishes, phone calls, and homework, or hurrying to get from point A to point B before the big hand on the clock reaches point C, what my brain often lets go of first is whatever my child is saying in the midst of the whirlwind. I've caught myself mindlessly saying yes to such ridiculous questions as: "Mom, can I eat candy for supper?" simply because I wasn't paying attention. I'm also guilty of agreeing to play a game or bring down a toy from a high shelf "just as soon as I finish doing this," only to realize 20 minutes later that I've failed to keep my word to my child because I was distracted with other chores. Equally disappointing are those times when I've made mistakes, even dragging my children in the wrong direction (or in my case, even into the wrong car!) because I didn't take the time to listen intently to what they were saying.

Our children need to know we're listening. At certain ages, we wish our children would talk a tad less to us, like when they're telling us 50 times a day, "I want to watch Barney." But as they grow older, we eventually wish they hadn't stopped talking, because we want to stay informed with the details of their lives. When we take the time to look into our children's eyes, put down the work of our hands, and stand at ease as they talk to us, they will know that we value what they have to say. And as we listen, we will glean insights into their worlds that will help us know how to pray for them, how to counsel them, and what God is doing in their lives. Furthermore, when we refuse to get distracted and we choose to pay close attention to our families and our surroundings, we are much more capable as mothers to make wise choices.

Listen carefully to your children today. You will affirm to them their great worth in your sight, and you'll find yourself engaging your children on a whole new level. And who knows, it might save you from embarrassment in the parking lot.

Heavenly Father, I want to be a better listener. Forgive me for those times when I've neglected my child's need to talk. Help me to wrap my attention around his thoughts today. Amen.

Reflection questions:

1. How would your child rate your level of interest in her words? What are the greatest distractions during your day?

2. How do you feel when someone listens intently to what you have to say?

3. Compare the following verses that challenge you to be a listener when God is speaking.
   Proverbs 8:34

   Ecclesiastes 5:1

   Isaiah 51:1

   Luke 8:15

"We celebrate our children's spiritual birthdays. We have a special family dinner, followed by a 'spiritual' birthday cake that I make. Gifts include Christian CDs, Bibles, books, or some token to remind them of their commitment to the Lord. We also spend time talking about their relationship with the Lord and how they've grown in Him over the years."
Cathy Warren, missionary, International Mission Board

Shall I come to you with a rod, or in love and a spirit of gentleness?
(1 Corinthians 4:21)

Rearview Reflections

It was the sort of day requiring survival chocolate. I was very pregnant and facing several errands with my three-year-old Julia and one-year-old Jay. I paused that morning to gain strength from God's Word. As I read 1 Corinthians 4:21, I cringed. "Lord, are You trying to tell me my children are going to tear me out of the frame today?" I prayed for patience and dreaded what the day might have in store.

The first stop was the adoption lawyer's office to complete Jay's adoption. I fastened Jay in the stroller, warned Julia to behave, and walked in the office with a tranquil smile to make a good impression. Minutes later, Jay released a blood-curdling scream. I turned (as did everyone else) to see my adopted son hanging from his stroller with his head inches from the tile floor; Julia stood close by wearing a guilty expression. My hormone-raging body struggled for restraint, but God's Word came to mind and I exercised patience.

In an attempt to brighten the day, I stopped at a restaurant for lunch. I propped my swollen feet up and enjoyed the silence as my children licked butter from their dinner rolls. What could spoil lunch? Jay soon ruined the ambiance with an unpleasant odor. My unborn son then got into the act, using my bladder for a trampoline.

We finished our meal and headed to the car. As I watched my daughter's ponytail bounce and I listened to Jay still chewing fries, I remembered 1 Corinthians 4:21 and resolved once again to be patient. I brought Jay's face close to mine as I bent down to change his diaper in the van. At that precise moment of face-to-face cuddling, Jay sneezed, propelling wet french fry all over my face and hair.

As I finished the diaper change, I asked a question in my head that shocked even me. "Lord, is it worth it?" Me—a woman who prayed for years to have a child before God opened my womb, who was overwhelmed with gratitude for the opportunity to adopt a child, and now very unexpectedly blessed with a third bundle on the way—for an instant, I couldn't help but wonder if motherhood, with all of its embarrassing thrills, loss of bladder control, and wet french fry hair, could be worth it all.

I buckled myself in and looked into my rearview mirror. Julia and Jay had already found something to giggle about, and they looked at me with dancing eyes filled with love. For a brief moment, I saw the image of God in my children's faces. Yes, in the reflection of my rearview mirror, I could see that motherhood would always be worth it.

How you handle frustrations will have an impact on your children's interactions with frustrating people, and people who need to know about Christ can be particularly frustrating at times! Just as motherhood is worth all of the trials because of the beautiful process of watching your children grow, developing relationships with lost people is also worth all of the trials because of the eternal blessing of seeing someone come to know Jesus as Savior. Are you teaching your children love and gentleness in relationships?

Draw strength from God's Word each morning. God knows what kind of day you're facing, and He will give you the encouragement you need to get through those difficulties if you'll open your Bible and allow Him to speak to you. When you feel like you're about to explode with frustration, consider the investment you're making in your child's life, and thank God for the great worth of your little one, made in the image of God.

Father, Help me to carve out enough time each day to be fed and strengthened by Your Word. I need Holy Scripture to keep me grounded and strong each day. I want to be a patient mother, handling aggravations with love and gentleness for the sake of my child, as well as to model before him how to handle frustrations in a godly manner. Amen.

Reflection questions:

1. When was the last time God gave you a specific Scripture to help you through a difficult situation?

2. How can you apply God's gentleness to your style of discipline? As you consider how to reflect the Father's ways in your parenting, how does God treat us with gentleness yet still make His point to wield change in our lives? (Hint: Think about the story of Jonah for a great example of God's gentleness applied in disciplining one of His children.)

3. Read James 3:17 as a measure for wise motherhood. How would the characteristics described in this verse help a kingdom-minded mother raise kingdom-hearted kids? Try to apply each characteristic to kingdom-heartedness.

"I'm learning to pay attention and not miss the opportunity to speak truth to my children. Seeing a dead squirrel turns into a conversation about 'death,' then to Nana who has gone to heaven, and then to how they can get to heaven. Ordinarily, I would have been busy or preoccupied."
Sandy Spence, local outreach coordinator, Cedar Creek Church, Aiken, South Carolina

And the man said to me, "Son of man, look with your eyes and hear with your ears, and fix your mind on everything I show you; for you were brought here so that I might show them to you."
(Ezekiel 40:4)

Life Applications in a Time-Out Chair

Every mom is a teacher, and a crucial element of teaching is helping your child apply knowledge. When I taught my daughter about colors, we sat in the rocking chair and pored through books, pointing to objects and naming the colors. However, when we shut the books and walked away, the lesson had just begun; we pointed at the colors in God's beautiful world throughout the day, reinforcing what we had learned in the books. Not only was Julia learning about colors, she was also learning about transferring knowledge into every life situation.

I've always been proud of Julia's ability to make spiritual applications, but occasionally she veers off in the wrong direction, reminding me to give a more thorough explanation during our next lesson. One evening while we watched the news, Julia was disturbed by the images of violence in the Middle East. "Mommy, why are those men hurting other people?" I tried to explain to her that many people don't have Jesus in their hearts, and that sometimes those people act mean and hurt others. The next Sunday morning, Julia went to Sunday School, and one of the minister's sons landed in time-out for hitting another child. Julia promptly marched over to the corner where he sat and announced in front of everyone to the minister's son, "You know, my momma says the reason why you act so mean is because you do not have Jesus in your heart!" My cheeks turned bright red as Julia's Sunday School teacher giggled through telling me about Julia's announcement. Yes, I suppose what she was describing was indeed what I had been talking about—the effects of original sin—but I never envisioned her applying that knowledge so forcefully on a little boy, let alone the minister's son!

God will bring experiences to eyewitness and sounds to hear for the sake of your child's spiritual growth. As you enjoy learning from devotionals, Bible studies, or impromptu teachable moments with your child, end those times with a private prayer between you and God, asking Him to help your child seize each opportunity to apply those spiritual truths. The application may come in a life experience within your family, in the life of a friend, or perhaps even in a story on television or in a book. Challenge yourself and your child to be spiritually alert so that neither of you miss out on the application moments of life.

Heavenly Father, I am moved that You must tell me to see with my eyes, and hear with my ears; how easily I can miss seeing You in the everyday moments of life! Realizing that it's in the classroom of the world that I and my child will apply Your wisdom, help me to be aware of application moments for myself and for my child. Amen.

Reflection questions:

1. Has there been a defining moment in your life when you gained a heightened understanding of a particular attribute of God (such as love, forgiveness, or mercy) through personal application? What happened? Have you shared this story with your child?

2. Is there something you want to teach your child about God, but you feel like your child will struggle to understand it? Pray about that piece of wisdom, and ask God to give you a plan to teach that lesson to your child with a powerful, life-changing impact.

3. Helping your children apply spiritual truths requires you as a mother to be disciplined and alert. Meditate on Psalm 119:37, and spend time in prayer.

"We really work at making good use of the teachable moments that are presented to us—seeing those golden nuggets of time that God lays at your feet to edify your children—and then taking the time to actually have a meaningful conversation. Kids need to see and hear us actively walking the walk—especially in today's world."
Liz James

Rest in the L*ORD*, *and wait patiently for Him. Do not fret—it only causes harm.*
(Psalm 37:7, 8)

Never Let Them See You Sweat

I spend a lot of energy thinking about my children. I want them to have positive childhood experiences, and I wonder if they're getting enough calcium. I worry they don't exercise enough, and I feel guilty because I can't cook like my mother. I listen to other mothers talk, and I notice that we moms can feel such heavy pressure to raise our children well.

The expression "never let them see you sweat" tells us to stay cool under pressure for the sake of appearance, but we a have spiritual reason not to worry at all: God is trustworthy! And according to the psalmist, my fretting only causes harm. Who am I harming? I'm likely doing damage to my health when I fret, and I notice that my head throbs and my stomach hurts. I'm also hurting my children, who are counting on me to provide assurance to their young hearts. And when I fret, I'm definitely damaging my witness before them as they look to me as a living testimony of the peace available through Jesus Christ.

What do you fret about? Do you stay troubled about people at work, your health, or your children's behavior? Or do you worry about less personal issues—injustice, the prosperity of evildoers, and the downward spiral of moral decay in the world? Regardless of what's got you wringing your hands, your fretting in no way betters the situation; it only causes more harm.

Isn't it a lovely invitation, to rest in the Lord? You don't have to wait until all of the world's problems are solved before you can rest in the Lord—you can rest in Him from moment to moment because you believe He is trustworthy. God invites you to say good-bye to fretting and patiently watch for His mighty hand to intervene in every situation, from potty training setbacks to failing grades in algebra.

As you approach your today and consider your tomorrows, fretting or resting in the Lord is your choice. Your decision will affect your children, either pointing them to our trustworthy God, or causing harm.

Father, it's difficult for me to be patient when I see problems all around me. I sometimes put pressure on myself to fix every problem. Help me to rely on Your trustworthiness today. I want to rest in You. Amen.

Reflection questions:

1. Try to notice every time you worry about your children today. Determine if you're fretting over their well-being, or if you're concerned about how their actions are affecting you. If pride is prompting you to fret, ask God to forgive you of that sin and to help you overcome prideful worries.

2. Read Luke 10:41–42. Like Martha, has your worried and troubled mind become distracted from prayer and the growth of your personal relationship with Christ?

3. Read the following verses, and spend time in prayer to heed their instruction. How will you teach these principles to your children?

   Philippians 4:6

   1 Peter 5:7

"I wanted to teach our two young daughters to look for and appreciate God's blessings. Each evening I asked them to express gratitude to God for something new from that day. This tradition became very special as they shared a new blessing they had encountered during the day."
Joy Brown, author and speaker (www.wordsofjoy.org)

"He who believes in the Son has everlasting life; and he who does not believe the Son shall not see life, but the wrath of God abides on him."
(John 3:36)

Scratch and Sniff

I've got one of those inquisitive little ones who constantly challenges me to explain deep theology on a level for someone still mastering the alphabet. Have you ever tried to explain the Holy Trinity to a chatty preschooler? It's tough.

One day Julia was grilling me about hell. She wanted to know all the gory details, and I was struggling to describe hell with the vivid imagery of the Bible without feeding her nightmare material. My biggest points of emphasis were, *It's hot, it's real, and it's very stinky.* Later that day, I was changing one of Julia's baby brother's diapers, and it was a doozy. Julia's eyes suddenly widened as if she had just had a great epiphany. "Momma," she said, "does hell smell as bad as my baby brother's diapers?"

"Yes, baby, and even worse than a dirty diaper."

Julia stuck her hands in the air like she was testifying to the congregation. "Well, then, I want no part of hell!" It was then that I realized that I was holding in my hands one of the greatest evangelistic tools ever known to mankind: a dirty diaper! For months, I had been throwing them away, when I could have been giving people a whiff of preparation for what their hardened hearts are in for if they continue to reject the Savior. I shared this idea with my Bible study group, and someone suggested that carrying soiled diapers around would be too messy and not practical for evangelism. I had to agree. She then suggested we create scratch and sniff stickers to attach to the back of gospel tracts. I thought the idea was a winner!

When children are young, we want to give them a big picture understanding of God's redemptive plan for mankind, and then we gradually begin to fill in the details. Sometimes we have to go a little out of order, like when a four-year-old wants the facts about the Trinity, but God guides us as mothers to know the timing of teaching deeper concepts of the Christian faith. We find it a joy to talk about God's faithfulness, His love and His promises, and the amazing life of Jesus Christ, but are we reluctant to talk about the not-so-pleasant realities of sin, death, suffering, and hell? To appreciate forgiveness, children must know about the filthiness of their sins. To comprehend life, they must understand death. To embrace God's calling on their lives, they must have a proper perspective of suffering for Christ. And to fully grasp the reality of heaven, they must know that God's Word describes an equally real and eternal place called hell.

Think about where you are in teaching the "big picture" to your children. As you start to fill in some of the details, enjoy sharing with your child the beauty and love of God and His plan; use broad, sweeping strokes of rainbow colors to paint the vividness of the glory of God! But don't neglect to paint the rain clouds and lightning, and with the Holy Spirit's help, guide your children to understand the realities of evil and the consequences of sin. Take a moment to linger there yourself, and allow those hard truths to ignite your sense of urgency to share Christ with a lost world.

Heavenly Father, when I look at my precious children, I wish I could shelter them from the harsh realities that come from living in this fallen world. Please grant me spiritual sensitivity to know how to inform my children about such painful topics as death and hell. God, may it make their hearts tender toward the people in this world who need Jesus. Amen.

Reflection questions:

1. What is your child's favorite Bible story? What does your child find most appealing about God? What is your favorite thing to share with your child about God?

2. When faced with a death near to your family, have you been tempted to tell your child that all people, pets, etc., go to heaven? What is the danger in giving this quick answer?

3. In John 3:16, perhaps the Bible verse most widely quoted for evangelism, Jesus alludes to hell. The emphasis is heavily placed upon God's love and His gift of salvation through Jesus, but the Lord includes the truth about the future for those who reject Him. Spend time thanking God for sparing you through Jesus Christ from an eternity in hell, and seek God's wisdom for explaining this powerful verse to your child.

"If I could relive my life, I would devote my entire ministry to reaching children for God!"
Dwight L. Moody, evangelist

And you have forgotten the exhortation which speaks to you as to sons: "My son, do not despise the chastening of the Lord, *nor be discouraged when you are rebuked by Him; for whom the* Lord *loves He chastens, and scourges every son whom He receives." If you endure chastening, God deals with you as with sons.*
(Hebrews 12:5–7)

With All My Heart

As I stood at the kitchen sink to finish up the dishes, I was lost in my thoughts while I scrubbed food off the plates. *Had I handled the situation properly? And what should I do now?* Julia was very angry with me because I had confiscated two of her rings, the trinkets she had chosen to play with instead of obeying my bedtime instructions. The evening had been filled with similar episodes of her playing instead of obeying her parents, and she was finally receiving consequences for her actions. Julia announced through her tears that she was angry with me for taking her rings. *She has the right to express her feelings,* I thought, but I calmly walked her through the events that had led up to her losing the rings. "I love you with all of my heart, Julia, and I want you to learn to obey me the first time you're asked to do something."

"Mommy, I thought I loved you with all of my heart, but now I think I was wrong. I don't love you that much." The words pierced my heart. Though they were spoken in haste by a five-year-old, the pain had lodged into my chest and was still throbbing while I stood over the sink.

Perhaps I was too harsh on her. No, she had been given several warnings. Besides, the two plastic rings were valued at 2.5 cents each, and she would get them back in the next few days. Should I go upstairs and tell her that I love her no matter how she feels about me, and guilt her into an apology? Should I refuse to fix her a nice breakfast in the morning to let her know she injured me? Somehow, neither option seemed like the course of action Jesus would take.

I wish I didn't have to do tough parenting, I thought, and then I talked with God about what I should do. God reminded me that He and Julia would go through similar tests of their relationship; as Julia grows in her faith as a Christian one day, there will likely be times when she will have to pay consequences for her poor decisions. If

I allow Julia to determine her capacity to love me based upon how she judges my decisions as her authority figure, will she decide one day that she loves God less when difficult consequences or circumstances arise? Then I thought about a little boy somewhere in the world who was also tucked in his bed that night, the little fellow who will one day be my son-in-law. Yes, he would thank me for not reinforcing in Julia this childish concept that her depths of love can change quickly if she is displeased with someone's actions.

You are training a child in the early years to prepare her for adulthood. The training process can be painful, but you're shaping your child's heart and mind to respond to adult-sized problems by practicing now on child-sized ones. As you make decisions about disciplining techniques and how to respond to character flaws in your child, look toward her future as you handle each situation. If Christ is to have lordship in your child's life, she will have to learn to submit willingly, even when serving God isn't fun and things don't turn out the way she expected. She must learn that in good times and in bad, she is called upon to love the Lord her God—with all her heart.

Father, I want my children to love me and even like me, and it hurts when they react harshly to my discipline. Help me to keep a proper perspective on their rejection of my firm hand, remembering that they are in training to follow Your lordship in their lives. Amen.

Reflection questions:

1. When are you most tempted to give in when your children react negatively to your punishments? Why do you suppose God doesn't back away from His discipline in our lives when we begin to kick and scream: "It's not fair!"?

2. God has a specific plan for your child's life, and, yes, assuredly that plan includes some hardship for God's glory. Imagine that your child is an adult and facing a hardship in her life. She asks you why God is allowing this circumstance to happen. How would you respond?

3. Read Deuteronomy 6:5. Plan to talk with your child about what this verse means, including loving God even when she is being disciplined.

"God created family to be a nurturing environment for passing on Christian values, morals, and habits—climate control over the outside influences of world standards and views. What a wonderful plan God has put into place!"
Angie Quantrell, author of Families on Mission: Ideas for Teaching Your Preschooler to Love, Share, and Care

To everything there is a season, a time for every purpose under heaven.
(Ecclesiastes 3:1)

From Playpens to Car Keys

As I turned over the empty playpen, old cracker crumbs spilled onto the floor. I took one last look at the juice-stained fabric, and I packed away the pen, never to be played in again. I took a deep breath and sighed. An era of my life was over. First it was the baby swing, then the bottles, and now it had come to this. With nothing left but a handful of pacifiers and a stack of diapers, the signs of infancy were slipping away. My babies weren't babies anymore.

My mind traveled back to a conversation I had with my husband only weeks earlier, when we did some dreaming about the future. Our children are still young and need their parents close to home, but I told my husband that I look forward to the day when we can go on the missions field for extended periods of time, once our children are raised and living on their own. I was in no way implying that I don't thoroughly enjoy this season of motherhood, but God has given me a longing in my heart that I want to fulfill. As I packed away the playpen, I realized that the days of this season of motherhood are quickly slipping away. The moment was bittersweet. I felt the overwhelming reality of the brevity of time, and I thought about my life, what I had already done, and what God would call me to do in the days remaining. I thought about God's calling on the lives of my children, and how they must grow up to fulfill those callings.

Do you ever look forward to your children's independence, yet at the same time long to keep them babies forever? It seems to be an emotional struggle for many moms. Children are little for such a short period of time, and then it seems you blink and they're borrowing your car keys. Each stage of motherhood has its purpose by God's plan. As your children grow, they are drawing closer to the time when they will spread their wings and serve the Lord as men and women, and you, too, are drawing closer to a new season of having more time to serve God in new and different ways. Every season of motherhood has its highlights and its struggles, but each day is sweet when the heavenly Father showers your home with His love. Cherish yesterday, live in the present, and prayerfully anticipate the future, all for the glory of God.

God, it's as if I have a heightened sense of the passing of time as I watch my children grow. They change and grow up so quickly! Help me to cherish each moment, and to live in the present. Amen.

Reflection questions:

1. Are you enjoying your current season of motherhood? Why or why not?

2. As your children grow older, you will have more time to do ministry outside of your home, but what are you doing today to minister to others? Ask God to help you determine how to serve in the kingdom of God within as well as outside of the borders of your home.

3. Read Psalm 39:4–5. How do these verses encourage you to approach your mission for the Lord today?

"As a stay at home mother, I am sometimes bombarded with requests because 'I have lots of time,' but when my focus is on God and God-led activities, I should have the attitude of Nehemiah: 'I am doing a great work, so that I cannot come down' (Nehemiah 6:3)."
Rachel Wallace

Seek the LORD *while He may be found, call upon Him while He is near.*
(Isaiah 55:6)

Out of the Mouths of Babes

God has given me the blessed task of talking with women across the nation about spiritual revival. I have been in awe of the hand of God as He stirs the revival waters in the hearts of women across our land. As I study God's Word, speak, and pray about revival, as I look at the trends in American morality and worldviews, and as I observe global unrest, my spirit is overwhelmed at times with a burden for God's people to turn their faces toward heaven to live in holiness with obedience to God.

Restore, the music group I travel with for my ministry's women's revival tour, wrote a song about spiritual revival entitled, "Last Days." The chords are somber and the words grip my heart, drawing me into the gravity of our great spiritual drought in our nation today. My daughter has heard the song from my computer, and now I will often catch her singing the words as she goes about her day. I have to restrain myself not to make her stop, because it breaks my heart to hear those words coming out of her young mouth: "We are in the last days." As gripping as the message is out of the mouth of an adult, picture the image of a beautiful young girl singing in innocence about the impend ing tribulation to come as God pours out His wrath.

John wrote, "Little children, it is the last hour" (1 John 2:18). I am moved by his compassionate framing of such a serious piece of information: time is expiring. The message sobers any adult, but what does it mean for children? It means that children must be prepared to take up the mantle for Christ as the next generation of warriors for the kingdom of God. It means they must learn to have a sense of urgency for the lost to find Jesus. It means they must be trained to live as Christ and not as the world, learning at a young age that we are on this earth to do the will of God, not to seek pleasure. It means their faith must be strengthened and anchored in Christ, because they are growing up in perilous times (2 Timothy 3:1).

No one knows if Christ will return tomorrow or 3,000 years from now, but we can be sure of this: we are closer to the Lord's return today than we were yesterday. Our children's generation will march further into the end times than we will, if the Lord tarries. Let us live joyfully, let peace reign in our hearts, and may we submit to the influence of the seriousness of the hour. May our children seek the Lord while He may be found.

Dear Lord, I know that You are coming again. Please don't let me lose sight of my purpose on this earth, and help me to impart that message to my children. Amen.

Reflection questions:

1. Write down your understanding of God's great purposes for your life.

2. Have your children accepted Jesus as Lord and Savior? If not, pray for them to seek the Lord. Ask God what He would have you to do to help your child.

3. Spend time in prayer for your children's futures. In this last era of time, called "the last days" in Scripture, spiritual hardships are described as being destructive and widespread. Pray for your children to be mighty soldiers of the cross.

"When our oldest son, Ben, was two, he had memorized many Scriptures. One day when I was particularly rushed and impatient, he looked up at me matter-of-factly and said: 'But the fruit of the spirit is love, joy, peace, patience, goodness, kindness, gentleness, and self-control.'"
Jennifer Weaver

Closing Thoughts for *Soul Shaping*

As I thought over the events of a recent missions trip to India, I tried to retrace the spiritual lessons God had taught me. I remembered singing praise to Him in the dark places of spiritual oppression. I could recall looking into the eyes of the Hindu pundit and realizing he was not to be feared, but he was a mother's son in need of salvation. Memories flooded my mind of the power of intercessory prayer. Then I recalled how often I started my day putting on the armor of God listed in Ephesians 6:13–17 because the warfare was very evident every day while I ministered in India.

Then my mind flipped to the challenges of my current home situation. Julia was beginning to show signs of selfishness, Jay was struggling with self-control, and my baby John Mark had recently begun to exercise a newfound stubborn streak. The Holy Spirit created the link for me as I processed these two ministry endeavors—missions in India and mothering my children—so closely together. To be an effective mom, I need to put on the armor of God. I need my waist girded with truth to provide my children a solid foundation of biblical principles. I must have the breastplate of righteousness to discipline my children with love and equity. I need my feet shod with preparation of the gospel to point my children to Jesus even in the midst of a long talk about sharing toys, or thankfulness even when we don't get our way. I must carry the shield of faith, because the enemy will try to rob me of the joy of motherhood with his fiery darts of discouragement. And the helmet of salvation—it is in Jesus Christ that I will be the best mother I can be.

Motherhood is many lofty and pleasant things, and it is also a spiritual battle. As mothers, we are waging war against the evil one for the welfare of our children, and also for our personal victory in Jesus Christ in this role of parenting. If we are to choose not only to raise children to love Jesus but also to adopt a missions lifestyle, we can expect greater opposition from the enemy. But we needn't fear, because "we are more than conquerors through Him who loved us" (Romans 8:37). We can win this battle because we are on the side of God, and the victory indeed will be sweet.

Love with your whole heart, discipline with tenacity, linger in prayer, and live it. Live the life you long for your children to experience. Be a kingdom-minded mom. May God bless your kingdom heart!

The Prayers of a Kingdom-Minded Mom

Praying the Word of God is a sure way to pray in agreement with God. These prayer prompts are just a small listing of the many ways you can pray for your child by personalizing Scripture.

1. Salvation through Jesus Christ (Romans 6:23; John 14:6)
   Father, please draw my child through the Holy Spirit. Convict and convince my child that Jesus is the Way, the Truth, and the Life.

2. Growth into spiritual maturity (Colossians 1:9–11)
   Lord, help my child to grow more and more into the image of Christ each day. Please grant my child spiritual strength, wisdom, and discernment.

3. Focus on the things of God (Romans 8:5–6)
   Set my child's heart toward the things of God, focusing on those things that are eternal. Give my child a longing for more of You.

4. Love for God's Word (Jeremiah 15:16)
   Grant my child a deep love for the Bible, Father.

5. Hunger and thirst for righteousness (Proverbs 23:12; Matthew 5:6)
   Lord, help my child to yearn for righteousness and to desire to please You as Lord and Savior.

6. Resolve to be above reproach (Psalm 19:13; Daniel 1:8; Romans 6:12)
   May my child walk in integrity all the days of his orher life.

7. Willingness to give cheerfully (2 Corinthians 9:6–8)
   Please give my child a desire to give generously to help others and to build Your kingdom.

8. Full surrender to God's will (Romans 12:1–2)
   Father, teach my child to listen to Your voice alone as a faithful guide; help my child to adopt Your great plan as the perfect plan for life.

9. Understanding of identity in Christ (Ephesians 2:19–22)
   Lord, may my child see his or her identity completely through Your eyes, knowing the eternal worth of a surrendered servant of Christ.

10. Submission to the authority of God and others (Romans 13:1–5; James 4:7)
    Please grant my child a willingness to submit to authority figures, especially to the authority of You, Father.

11. A life that glorifies God in all things (1 Corinthians 6:20; John 15:8)
    May the life of my child glorify You in every way, dear Lord.

12. A commitment to pray fervently (Philippians 4:6–7)
    Teach my child to pray, Lord, and to stay in close communication with You.

13. A thankful spirit (1 Thessalonians 5:18)
    Grant my child the ability to see your blessings in all things, and to give thanks to You.

14. Deep faith in the Living God (Proverbs 29:25; Isaiah 26:3; Nahum 1:7)
    May my child's faith run deep, Lord; may he or she act on this faith in the moment-by-moment decisions of life.

15. A humble attitude in service to God (Mark 9:33–35)
May my child serve You with an attitude of a grateful and humble servant, bringing glory to the Master.

16. Sweet fellowship with Jesus (1 Corinthians 1:9; Revelation 3:20)
Help my child to sense the many ways You invite him or her to draw near, and to enjoy sweet fellowship with You.

17. A strong work ethic (Proverbs 13:4; Ecclesiastes 9:10)
Please grant my child strong arms, a sharp mind, and a desire to work hard to honor You and bless others.

18. Belief in the power of God (Mark 9:23)
Lord, please give my child a deep belief in Your great power to move mountains, and may that belief cheer him or her each day.

19. Christian relationships (Proverbs 27:17; Ecclesiastes 4:9–10)
Please plant Christian teachers, mentors, friends, and a Christian mate for my child according to Your great timing.

20. Purity (Psalm 24:3–4; Matthew 5:8; 1 Thessalonians 4:3–7)
Help my child to value purity as a means of honoring You.

21. A content heart (1 Timothy 6:6; Hebrews 13:5–6)
Lord, teach my child the value of being content in all things, able to thrive cheerfully with whatever good gifts You send his or her way.

22. A strong voice for the gospel message (Acts 4:7–13, 18–20)
May the gospel message stay on the lips of my child, spoken with passion and conviction.

23. A deep understanding of the world's plight (Matthew 9:36–38)
Allow my child to see the world through Your eyes, God.

24. A desire for missions (Psalm 96:3)
May my child be one who declares Your glory to the nations, Lord!

25. Joy in service (Nehemiah 12:43; Psalm 100:2)
May joy abound in the heart of my child as he or she serves You, regardless of the circumstances of life.

26. Fruitfulness (John 15:16)
May everything my child does in Your name bring forth fruit for Your glory.

27. Love for the people of God (John 13:35; 1 John 4:7)
Pour Your love into my child's heart to love the family of God.

28. Love for the lost sheep (Luke 15:4–7; John 21:15–17)
Help my child to love the lost of this world with the love of Christ.

29. Courage that knows no bounds (Deuteronomy 31:6; Ezra 10:4)
Father, I pray that my child will be courageous in all things according to Your great truths strengthening him or her.

30. Spiritual vision (Job 42:5; Ezekiel 40:4)
Please give my child eyes to see Your leadership and Your glory.

Five Simple Ways to Expose Your Children to God's Missions Field

1. **Take a prayer drive.** Pop in a worship CD and encourage your children to see their community through God's eyes. Pray aloud together, asking God to help you see the needs in your community as well as the opportunities for ministry. As your children share their ideas about how God is at work in the people and places you pass along your drive, pray for these needs. Follow up on any ministry need that sparks a particular interest in your children.
Preschooler Option: Select a location such as a hospital, church, or school to visit with your child. Talk about the wonderful ways God helps us at that particular location, and thank God for the people who help us too. (For instance, thank God for doctors and nurses.) Tell your child that God is sharing His love with people all the time, even in these special places in your town.

2. **See the souls.** Take your children to a location where people pass by, like an outdoor café or a park. Set a short time frame based on the ages of your children, perhaps three to five minutes, to do this exercise. Challenge your children to quietly watch the people walking by, and to think about how each person was created by God, is known and loved by God, and needs to know that Jesus died for their sins. After the time frame is up, talk with your children about what their thoughts were about the people walking past them. Encourage them to begin seeing everyone as a person that God loves and to pray for the people they know who need Jesus.
Preschooler Option: Sit together at a distance to watch the people, and allow your children to tell you about the people they see. Then say together, "God loves the lady in the bright green shirt!"

3. **Understand poverty.** Along with your children, select a blessing your family enjoys that would be considered a luxury in an impoverished family, such as electricity, running water, or toys. For a short period of time, choose not to indulge in that luxury. As you and your children run into obstacles because of the loss of that blessing, talk about what it would be like to live without the many other things you may take for granted. Talk about how much God loves the poor and wants us to help others in need.
Preschooler Option: Take your children to your food pantry in your kitchen, and talk about the different types of food you have in your house. Allow them to tell their favorite foods. Then let them help you take all of the food out of the pantry, except for one type of food, such as potatoes. Talk about what mealtime would be like if your family only had one type of food to eat. Then empty the pantry completely, and talk about the hungry families of the world who don't have food. Pray for people who are needy. As you return your food to the pantry, fill up some bags of groceries to take to a local charity food pantry.

4. **Get global.** Introduce your children to the sights, sounds, smells, and tastes of different countries. Enjoy ethnic festivals, visit missions Web sites together, sit down with children's atlas books, and be intentional about learning about other cultures. Be sure to include information about the religious beliefs of people of other countries. Allow your children to help you with an ethnic recipe from the country you're studying, and pray for the people of that country during your blessing for that meal.
Preschooler Option: Begin exposing your young children to the idea that the world is very big, and that people around the world live in many different ways. Rather than focusing on particular countries, show your children pictures of different types of houses, styles of dressing, transportation, and other cultural differences. Play dress up by attempting to use things in your closet to dress like

the people of different countries. Say a prayer of thanks that God makes every person special, and loves us all the same.

5. **Write it down.** Begin a prayer journal with your children. Decide which categories you would like to pray for, such as sick people, friends and family who need Jesus, missionaries, personal concerns, and the people of a people group or country who do not know Jesus as the Son of God. Fill in the journal together, including the date added and the date the prayer is answered. Discuss with your children how you can best pray for those needs. For instance, you may decide not only to pray for the lost people of China, but to pray for the people who live in a certain village or for a city of people who are suffering from a natural disaster.
Preschooler Option: Make a collage of the people you would like to pray for using your child's drawings, photos, or pictures from a magazine. Include prayer for the people in your community and around the world who need to know about God's love.

Also by Kimberly Sowell

A Passion for Purpose

365 Daily Devotions for Missional Living

Kimberly Sowell, Edna Ellison, Joy Brown, Tricia Scribner, Marie Alston

ISBN-13: 978-1-59669-242-8

Women of the Covenant

Spiritual Wisdom

from Women of the Bible

Kimberly Sowell and Edna Ellison

ISBN-13: 978-1-59669-270-1

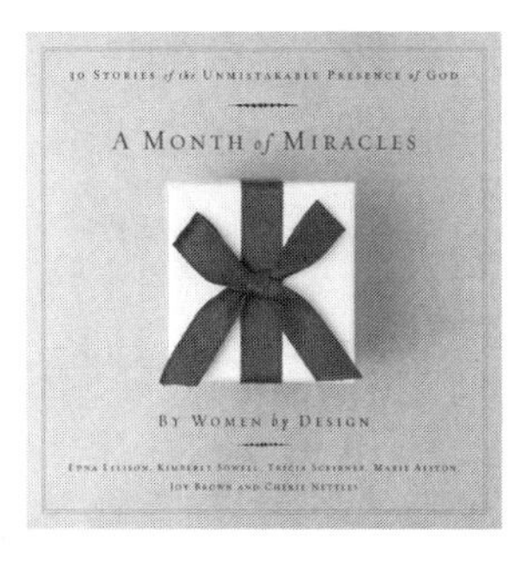

A Month of Miracles

30 Stories of the

Unmistakable Presence of God

Kimberly Sowell, Edna Ellison, Joy Brown,

Tricia Scribner, Marie Alston, and Cherie Nettles

ISBN-13: 978-1-59669-209-1

Journey to Significance

Becoming Women

of Divine Destiny

Kimberly Sowell

ISBN-13: 978-1-59669-217-6

New Hope® Publishers is a division of WMU®, an international organization that challenges Christian believers to understand and be radically involved in God's mission. For more information about WMU, go to www.wmu.com. More information about New Hope books may be found at www.newhopepublishers.com. New Hope books may be purchased at your local bookstore.

If you've been blessed by this book, we would like to hear your story. The publisher and author welcome your comments and suggestions at: newhopereader@wmu.org.